HIKING TRAILS of SOUTHERN IDAHO

The author

HIKING TRAILS of SOUTHERN IDAHO

by
S. R. BLUESTEIN

The CAXTON PRINTERS, Ltd.
Caldwell, Idaho
1981

Library of Congress Cataloging in Publication Data

Bluestein, S   R
   Hiking trails of Southern Idaho.

   Bibliography: p.
   1. Hiking—Idaho—Guide-books. 2. Back packing—
Idaho—Guide-books. 3. Idaho—Description and travel—
1951-   —Guide-books. I. Title.
GV199.42.I2B58   917.96   79-52543
ISBN 0-87004-280-7

Lithographed and Bound in the United States of America by
The Caxton Printers, Ltd.
Caldwell, Idaho 83605
135429

CONTENTS

ILLUSTRATIONS

INTRODUCTION

Idaho offers outstanding opportunities for wilderness hiking. The Gem State has five National Forest Wilderness Areas, including America's two largest, the Selway-Bitterroot and River of No Return Wilderness Areas. The Forest Service also studied another two hundred roadless areas in its Roadless Area Review and Evaluation (RARE II) and recommended that fifteen new wilderness areas be established. While the Bureau of Land Management has just begun to survey its vast desert roadless areas, several are already earmarked for intensive study. Most of these areas truly fit the definition of wilderness as "the America that was . . . where the earth and its community of life are untrammeled by man."

The state's 17,835-mile trail system can meet the needs of every hiker. There are "highways" in the Sawtooth Wilderness for beginners and "manways" in the Selway-Bitterroot Wilderness for experts. There are small, intimate areas close to civilization like Cottonwood Creek, and huge, rarely traveled regions at road's end such as the River of No Return Wilderness. There are intensive areas of jagged, glacier-carved peaks like the Sawtooth Range, and extensive areas of deep valleys and rounded ridges like the Salmon River Mountains. And the best thing about Idaho's vast roadless areas is that they receive much less use than comparable areas in other states.

This does not mean that all is well in Idaho's backcountry. Pressure on the state's wild areas is increasing at a dramatic rate, and it is coming not only from wilderness foes but from friends, too. Developers, of course, seek to limit the quantity of wilderness. They want to exploit the state's dwindling timber and mineral resources, and road construction is a vital part of their program. Hikers themselves reduce the quality of wilderness. Their numbers have greatly increased due to Idaho's improved roads, her increased population, the tremendous backpacking boom of the 1970s, and national publicity given to Idaho's wilderness. The Forest Service is trying to settle the preservation/development issue through RARE II, which still has several areas in a "Further Planning" category. It may also try to settle the wilderness degradation issue with a permit system for heavily used areas.

However, the government cannot be expected or permitted to settle these problems by itself. Dedicated hikers must make themselves part of the solution. They need to join groups that fight for protection of the remaining wilderness and that monitor government resource utilization in nonwilderness areas. Also, hikers must act responsibly as individuals and use the backcountry with respect. They not only must shed old habits from bough-bed and lean-to days but must also learn new techniques of minimal-impact camping.

Hikers must realize that Idaho's backcountry is an irreplaceable resource. It can only gain in value as time goes on and technology increasingly dominates people's lives. Perhaps the Northern Rockies wilderness system will become an attraction of such worldwide importance as Kenya's wildlife resource. This wilderness system is the product of a period of affluence and leisure unprecedented in human history. Idaho hikers must use this resource so that future generations find in their wilderness legacy a reflection of our time's concern for the natural environment, and not just one more relic of a throwaway society.

SURVIVAL

Survival is usually thought of as a short-term problem involving a small number of people. Yet it is also a long-term problem affecting all mankind, for wilderness quality is a key to the quality of the environment as a whole. As a hiker you need to consider both aspects — can you survive the wilderness, and can the wilderness survive you? Do you have the skills to protect yourself and the environment?

Of course you must have adequate equipment to survive. But possession of the world's best equipment does not guarantee safe wilderness travel. In a true survival situation, when the odds of coming back alive are tilted against you, you must rely on the same piece of "equipment" that enabled man to rise to mastery over this world — your brain. If you employ common sense, you will:

1. Tell someone responsible where you are going and when you'll be out. (The Forest Service or good backpacking stores should be happy to log you out and in.)
2. Carry the Ten Essentials for Wilderness Travel (see page 15).
3. Travel in parties of at least two. (A party of four is safest, since an injured person can be cared for while a pair goes for help.)
4. Be aware that accidents happen to overconfident, careless intermediates more often than to beginners.
5. Realize that the expression "I promise" can get you into trouble, as in "I promise I'll be back at five."
6. Know that three of anything — whistles, fires, yells — is the international distress signal.
7. Stay with your shelter in bad weather. (You can survive three days without water and two weeks without food.)
8. Remember that hiking down most drainages in Idaho will bring you to a road or trail.
9. Understand that fear is a natural reaction to a survival situation — and that it can be channeled into activity that will enable you to survive.

You must employ not only common sense but skills to survive in the wilds. If you are a beginner, start your backpacking career slowly. First read one of the backpacking books in Appendix B. Try day hikes and overnight hikes before attempting longer trips. Do at least three hikes in each level of difficulty before advancing to the next level. And carefully read the rest of this chapter, which discusses skills needed to save both you and the wilderness.

You need to become skilled at protecting your food from varmints. And the varmints are out there! While bear trouble is rare in the backcountry, mouse trouble is common. You should expect problems every time you fail to safeguard food. The only solution is to take precautions *every* night. If you carry your food and cook kit in waterproof, drawstring ditty bags, you can hang the bags from nylon cord or tree branches. You can string the cord horizontally between two or three trees, tying the drawstrings to the cord (and using the cord for airing sleeping bags and drying out other gear in the morning). Or you can tie the bags to the end of the cord and suspend them from a high branch. If the improbable happens and the cord is gnawed through, you will at least hear your cook kit smash to the ground and be able to watch the bears eat your breakfast.

There are other critters out there waiting to get you, and you must be ready for them. The smallest are the microbes in contaminated water. Beaver, sheep, humans, and pack stock have poor sanitary habits, so water purification is *essential* on most hikes (see Appendix B for an article on water treatment). The next problem critter in size is the tick. Idaho averages sixteen cases of Colorado tick fever and three cases of the more severe Rocky Mountain tick fever each year. Symtoms of these tick-borne diseases appear in five to seven days and include fever, headache, body ache, and a rash. Untreated Rocky Mountain tick fever can be fatal, so early diagnosis is important. You should check for ticks at least once a day, especially in the spring. The last problem critter is the rattlesnake. The state has recorded no deaths due to rattlesnake bite in the last twenty-five years, and the fear these reptiles have aroused probably exceeds the actual pain and suffering they have caused. Treatment with cold and constriction is increasingly favored over cut-and-suck, but it is easier to carry a snakebite kit in the desert than a bag of ice. The key to avoiding all three critter hazards is prevention — treat your water, check for ticks, and watch for rattlers.

Now that you have safely survived your wilderness journey, consider how well the wilderness has survived *you.* Have you adequately disposed of your waste? Have you carried out all you carried in? Have you left such traces of your presence as fire rings where you cooked, fish guts and line where you fished, ditches where you pitched your tent, or cigarette butts and candy wrappers where you walked?

The Forest Service has perfected methods for wilderness sanitation and waste removal. For disposal of human waste, use a small digging tool such as a garden trowel (or an ice axe). Select a spot at least fifty feet from open water and dig a hole eight inches in diameter and six to eight inches in depth. Here is the "biological disposer" soil layer. After use, fill the hole with loose soil and then tramp in the sod. Camouflage the spot with pine needles, and nature will do the rest within a few days. In disposing of camp waste, you must carry out cans, bottles, *aluminum foil,* and anything else that will not burn. Cans are easier to carry out if they are scorched and flattened. Burying is not satisfactory because the cans and other garbage usually will be exposed by animal or frost action. Paper and other burnable

material may be burned in your campfire — or carried out if you don't use a fire.

The Forest Service has established other rules to minimize impact on heavily used wilderness areas. They include a limitation on group size to twenty persons, a prohibition on limbing or cutting live trees, and a requirement that campsites be restored to natural appearance upon leaving. One important technique for restoring natural appearances is that of eliminating fire rings. This simple skill should be used whenever you have made a fire ring where there was none before, or where there are too many in an area. When the ashes from your fire (preferably a small one) are cold, replace the rocks that surrounded the fire in their original setting with the blackened side down. Scatter any unburned fire wood. Dump the ashes and charcoal where they can't be seen, under brush or low trees. Take soil, pine needles, and twigs from the nearby ground and use them to cover the fire scar and make it appear normal. Use your imagination, have fun, and you'll be amazed at the results.

One of the most important survival tools you can carry is the backpacking stove. A small butane or white gas powered stove minimizes your effect on the wilderness by reducing scars on soil and rocks, loss of nutrients to the soil, and the chance of wildfire. And it maximizes your chance of survival when things go wrong. A quick drink of cocoa can revive you if you are suffering from exposure, give you the strength to reach the good campsite just over the ridge, or enable you to weather a severe storm. A stove gives you tremendous flexibility. It lets you camp where there is no firewood, permits you to cook dinner in your tent when it's raining outside, and enables you to quickly fix hot drinks along the trail on a cool day. It also lets you prepare a freeze-dried meal next to a creek in late afternoon so you can fill your canteens and hike to a high, dry, and wild campsite for the night. Purchase and carry a good stove! It will last practically forever, and in time yours will become a good friend you wouldn't think of camping without. A good stove is the key to minimal-impact camping.

Idaho's wilderness must be used responsibly if it is to keep its high quality. The slogan, "Pack out what you pack in" doesn't go far enough to maintain pristine backcountry areas. "Leave it cleaner and better than you found it" better expresses the commitment to an untrammeled wilderness that every user of this book must have. If those who hike the trails described in this guide follow this rule, then our tremendous wilderness resource will not be degraded but rather improved. And if they follow the commonsense rules for wilderness safety and survival, they will enjoy the beauties of Idaho's backcountry for many, many years.

EQUIPMENT

The weekend backpacker's equipment needs are fairly simple in Idaho's gentle wilderness. The purchase of expensive, sophisticated gear is unnecessary, since summer is usually dry and warm, and most campsites are sheltered by trees. Inexpensive tents and sleeping bags are adequate for most summer hiking, keeping your finances sound and your packs light. This section will give recommendations on sleeping systems, shelters, packs, boots, clothing, and other essential and nonessential items for Idaho backpacking.

You must have an adequate sleeping bag and insulating cushion under it for enjoyable camping. For Idaho summers your bag should have a minimum temperature rating near twenty degrees and should have temperature-regulating features such as full side zippers and drawstring hoods. In deciding on a bag your biggest choice will be between goose down and synthetic filling materials. Each type has its advantages and disadvantages.

Goose down sleeping bags work well in Idaho. Their biggest drawback, loss of loft and insulating ability when wet or damp, is rarely a problem in the mild summer climate. It is hard to recommend fill weights for down bags because designs and down quality vary. A narrow, true mummy bag with 1½ pounds of down should be adequate in the summer and perhaps into the fall. A wider, modified mummy bag with two or more pounds of fill would do the same job. Remember, though, that some people sleep cold and require more insulation than the army troops on whom the insulation charts are based! A high-quality goose down bag has one more drawback — its expense. But after you've slept one hundred nights in your $200 bag is costs only $2.00 per night — and that's not too much for all that luxury, is it?

The well-designed fiberfill sleeping bags now available can easily and cheaply fill the needs of the Idaho backpacker. Dacron's big advantage over goose down (superior performance in a wet environment) is not as important in dry Idaho as in wetter climes. Its big drawback (less insulation per pound fill) is not as important for the summer hiker who isn't worried about temperatures in the teens. Depending on bag design, two-and-a-half to three pounds of synthetic insulation should be adequate for summer. Fiberfills are more efficient and comfortable on the bottom of a bag than goose down, so a down top-fiberfill bottom bag is also a good choice.

A foam pad or air mattress is required for warm and comfortable sleeping in the wilds. There are many varieties of foam pads to choose from: short and long, narrow and wide, closed cell and open cell. You should choose for comfort. Of all the equipment decisions made by a friend for a three-week trip in the Primitive Area, the one she regretted most was the substitution of a thinner, lighter foam pad for her regular thick one. Air mattresses, the more traditional underbag cushions, do not insulate as well as foam pads, and they may leak. Some outstanding new designs minimize these problems, so if space in your pack is a problem then perhaps an air mattress is for you.

Next in importance to a good sleeping system is an adequate shelter. The requirements one must meet for summer camping are not demanding, since most trips are below timberline and in the shelter of the forest. High altitude (winter) tent designs are simply not necessary. Light rainfall means you don't even have to have a floor, although it is a luxury you'll enjoy on hot nights when you want to crawl halfway out of your bag. Protection against bugs and plans for use beyond summer are the critical factors in deciding just how much (or how little) tent you need.

Suitable shelters range from the lowly

tarp to the winter expedition tent. The tarp is the simplest, lightest, and cheapest. One with mosquito netting on the ends and a groundcloth or poncho underneath can do the job in forest areas. The tarp's big disadvantage is that it is not var-mintproof. Persistent mice have a way of entering tarp tents and jumping around all night (and even borrowing part of your sweater).

The next step up in shelters, the water-proof tent, overcomes most of the tarp's disadvantages. These inexpensive, made-in-East-Asia "backpacker tents" are widely available in discount and sporting goods stores. They have I-poles at each end, with no separate rainfly. They are adequate for most Idaho summer camping because their main defect, condensation of moisture on roof and wall, is not serious in dry weather. One with side and rear win-dows, mosquito netting door, and a floor will provide you with lightweight protec-tion against the elements and the var-mints.

A tent with a separate rainfly, though heavier, is the most comfortable and ver-satile shelter you can buy. One with fiberglass wands or aluminum A-frame poles will be sturdy under all conditions and can even be used for winter camping. With the fly in place, moisture passes out through the breathable inner tent. Thus condensation is not a problem, and rainy weather does not make water drip on your face all night — as can happen with waterproof tents.

An important variation on the rainfly tent is the mosquito netting tent. It has netting in the upper, breathing portion of the inner tent. On clear nights you have a view of the stars and a sense of closeness to nature that has proven scary to some. On threatening nights you can set up the rainfly halfway and in case of showers jump up, pull it over the tent, and leap back into your bag. The mosquito tent is not windproof enough for winter use but does a terrific job in the summer. In your choice of a shelter you must strike a bal-ance between your needs, your load-

carrying ability, your comfort, and your budget. Have fun!

And now for packs. The basic choice in packs is between a soft pack with an in-ternal frame and a hard pack with an ex-ternal frame. If you are strictly a weekend warrior with no ambition for longer trips, a soft pack may satisfy your needs. Make sure it has a hipbelt that takes the load off your shoulders. It should also have enough room for your tent poles and sleeping system. If you are interested in longer trips, a Kelty-type external frame pack will probably be necessary. These packs have been criticized in recent years, while internal frame designs and sales have flourished. One criticism has been that the external frame can get caught in branches and brush, but Idaho's trails are not very brushy. Another criticism has been that the packs do not ride closely enough to the body to provide positive control of the weight, that they can flop around and throw the hiker off-balance. This criticism is valid for some packs' sus-pension systems. Thoroughly check out any pack. Talk to owners and rent if possi-ble before you buy. In addition to your primary pack you may want to carry a small rucksack or belt pack with light weight and low bulk to carry the Ten Es-sentials on day hikes. Any difficulty you have in choosing between the different types of packs can be solved by buying one of each!

Your biggest choice in selecting boots is between a flexible-soled backpacking boot and a rigid-soled climbing boot. None of the hikes in this book requires a climbing boot, but the hiker who travels off the trails and carries heavy loads might find the extra support of the rigid sole more important than their extra weight and ex-pense. Moccasins or tennis shoes are lux-ury items that some weekend hikers may choose to carry. Wool socks can get itchy and uncomfortable in summer. Synthetic socks in either thin liner or thick main sock sizes can cure this problem. Be sure to break in new boots on short hikes be-fore starting on any long trips!

You must have the correct clothing to

fully enjoy the wilderness. You should be able to meet your shirt and pant needs with what you already have in your closet. Cutoffs or other shorts are fine for many summer days, but you must carry long pants for bug protection, bushwhacking stretches, and the evening cool. Many people hike in jeans, but lightweight, light-colored dacron-cotton pants are cooler and dry faster. Large pants pockets are not important, since the larger the pocket, the more you are tempted to put in it, and too much weight and bulk in pockets puts extra strain on your thighs. T-shirts are adequate for many summer days, but you must carry one good-quality, long-sleeved shirt for sun and mosquito protection and for cool evenings.

When it comes to outerwear, some special purchases may be necessary. The first essential is good raingear. A poncho keeps you dry and may double as a groundcloth. A rain parka with hood is more expensive but also protects against the wind and may do more duty in this role than in shedding rain. Rain pants are a luxury worth the expense. They can add warmth on a cold evening and act as armor against the mosquitoes. A goose down or dacron insulated garment is the second essential. Parkas are excellent and can be used in spring and fall, but a vest ought to be adequate for Idaho summer conditions. A vest along with a wool shirt or sweater is probably the most versatile combination for keeping you warm. Proper headgear is the third essential. A wool hat will keep you warm, and a cotton sun hat will protect you from sun and rain. A bandana should be carried to keep mosquitoes and flies out of your ears, to cool off your neck after you dip it in cool water, and to use as a washcloth.

Your miscellaneous equipment list is headed by the Ten Essentials for Wilderness Travel. They are:

1. Map. You should always carry a U.S. Geological Survey map of the area you are hiking. The maps in this book are intended as planning aids only; they are inadequate in the field.
2. Compass. You should carry a compass, preferably the lightest and cheapest Boy Scout model, as long as you think you need one. When you look at it and ask yourself, "Why do I carry this two ounces when I never use the thing and I know I only have to watch my drainages to stay found?" — on that day stop carrying it.
3. Flashlight. One is always needed for setting up tarp tents in pitch darkness and pouring rain. A penlight that can be carried in your shirt pocket is very handy.
4. Extra clothing. At the least you should always carry raingear and spare socks.
5. Sunglasses. These are needed in all seasons, but especially in the spring when you may encounter snow.
6. Waterproofed matches. One effective way of protecting matches for an emergency is to seal two books with a plastic bag sealer (of the Seal-a-Meal type). "Strike anywhere" matches often fizzle out at high altitudes and should be avoided.
7. Candle or fire starter. Candles have a tendency to melt in your pack in the summer. Army surplus hexamine tablets sealed in plastic make excellent emergency fire starters (and don't forget the fuel in your stove).
8. Extra food. Exactly how much extra food you need depends on your trip's duration and route.
9. Pocket knife. The thinner the knife, the better. Thick knives chafe your thigh and encourage you to carry in heavy and expensive wine bottles with corks.
10. First aid kit. Consult your doctor, and include lots of moleskin and Band-Aids for blisters.

There are many other items you should consider carrying into the mountains. They include toilet paper, the eleventh essential; insect repellent; suntan lotion or sunscreen; fifty feet of nylon cord; needle and thread; snakebit kit, for use in the wrong place at the wrong time; books, but not page-turners that make you forget about hiking; binoculars or monocular — and don't forget that, turned backward, these can be used for closeup nature study; camera, with extra film and a polarizing filter; thermometer, but don't leave yours hanging from a tree in a remote place; fishing tackle; ice axe — useful on rock as well as snow and almost essential as an aid to solo hiking; and a whistle — good for keeping a large party together and for signalling distress.

NATURAL HISTORY

An awareness of Idaho's climate, geology, and plant and animal life can help you plan and enjoy your wilderness outings. While these subjects are only outlined here, more information can be found in the book list in Appendix B.

Climate

South-central Idaho's climate is characterized by warm, dry summers dominated by the Pacific High, and by cool, wet winters dominated by the Aleutian Low. This weather pattern clearly favors the summer backpacker; rarely do the mountains get more than two or three days of bad weather in a row. Unfortunately, there are just two days in a weekend, and some summers it seems like the weeks are warm and dry and the weekends are cool and wet. Exceptions to the two-day rule seem to come in late May, early July, and mid-August, when entire weeks of wet weather often occur. Before entering the mountains you should listen carefully to weather forecasts and adjust your plans if necessary to avoid higher elevations and exposed places if the outlook is poor. A willingness to brave the elements in bad weather, including the snow that can fall in any month, can buy you some solitude in heavily used areas such as the Sawtooths. However, the solitude while you're waiting for the snow to melt is not the most enjoyable kind.

The charts that follow present critical weather data from six southern Idaho locations. The recording stations pinpointed in the index maps on pages 24-25, and 173, all lie in valleys that are warmer and drier than the mountains around them. Station elevation is given after the name, and you can assume that the temperature is roughly three degrees cooler for every one thousand feet of altitude gained above the valley. The charts give the following information: mean daily highs and lows, the normal temperatures you can expect; record highs and lows, to give you an idea of how bad things can get; total precipitation, to provide you with an idea of wetness or dryness; number of days with greater than one-tenth inch of precipitation, to give you your chances of getting rained on; and number of days with precipitation greater than one-half inch, to tell you your chances of getting rained out.

Geology

Idaho's geology is complex and varied, with northern, southern, eastern, and central Idaho forming distinct geologic realms. There is no up-to-date comprehensive book on the subject, though new 1:250,000 scale geologic maps (recently published by the Idaho Bureau of Mines and Geology) may spawn one. This section gives first an overview of Idaho geology and then a more complex treatment of the subject.

A vast uplift took place over much of central Idaho in Precambrian times, some 600 million years ago, raising sedimentary rocks which had been deposited in seas even earlier. In Paleozoic times, from 400 million to 600 million years ago, this uplift was reduced to a low plain by erosion, and parts of Idaho were again invaded by shallow seas. In late Mesozoic times, about 135 million years ago, a huge batholith (a mass of igneous rock which does not break the surface) rose, uplifting the vast plain, and began to push the sea out of Idaho. In Cenozoic times, beginning 60 million years ago, erosion removed most traces of the earlier plain from the top of the batholith while dividing it with great river systems. Also during this time many mountains were folded and faulted, especially in southeast Idaho. Beginning about 25 million years ago, great basalt flows covered low areas to the west, east, and south of the batholith, creating large lakes in southern Idaho. In more recent times glaciation has occurred in much of Idaho, carving the features that make the high peaks so exciting.

A more detailed history starts in the same time, the Precambrian era. Through much of this time most of the state was under water, although a few parts of south central Idaho remained above the seas. Most of Idaho's Precambrian rock formations are composed of metamorphosed sedimentary rocks. Some in our area include the Yellowjacket formation east of the Middle Fork of the Salmon River and also near Borah Peak; the Hoodoo quartzite, found above the Yellowjacket at the Middle Fork, at Borah, and near Yellow Pine; the Thompson Peak formation in the heart of the Sawtooths; the Hyndman and East Fork formations near Sun Valley; and the Green Creek complex and Elba quartzite near Independence Lakes. The trough in which these rocks were deposited was largely uplifted towards the end of the Precambrian era and then eroded.

Paleozoic times again saw the sea invade Idaho. The Cordilleran geosyncline covered varying areas of southeast Idaho for some 400 million years. The Sawtooth and Big Wood River valleys roughly mark the western border of this sea's advance. Major Paleozoic rocks are the Phi Kappa formation in the Pioneer Mountains and the Milligan and Wood River formations in the Boulder and White Cloud mountains. A full sequence of Paleozoic sedimentary rocks can be found in the Borah Peak area.

The oldest Mesozoic rocks in our area are the Seven Devils volcanics and the Casto volcanics of the late Permian and early Triassic. The biggest event of the Mesozoic, the emplacement of the Idaho batholith, began in the Cretaceous. This large mass of granodiorite covers some

Month	Mean High Temp.	Record High Temp.	Mean Low Temp.	Record Low Temp.	Total Precip. (Inches)	No. Days Greater Than 1/10″	No. Days Greater Than ½″
ARROWROCK DAM — 3,239′							
Mar.	48	81	27	−6	2.1	6	1
Apr.	61	88	36	8	1.5	5	1
May	70	96	43	26	1.1	3	+
June	78	108	49	32	1.1	3	+
July	91	112	56	39	.3	1	+
Aug.	90	106	55	36	.2	1	+
Sep.	79	105	46	24	.5	2	+
Oct.	64	89	37	17	1.2	4	1
IDAHO CITY — 3,950′							
May	69	95	34	17	1.9	6	1
June	77	106	39	24	1.4	3	1
July	89	109	44	26	.3	1	0
Aug.	87	105	41	24	.3	1	+
Sep.	79	100	34	11	.6	2	+
Oct.	47	91	28	9	1.6	3	1
McCALL — 5,025′							
May	60	90	33	14	2.4	8	1
June	68	94	40	20	2.0	5	1
July	81	102	45	26	.5	2	+
Aug.	78	104	42	23	.6	3	1
Sep.	69	94	35	9	1.2	3	1
Oct.	56	81	29	1	2.2	6	1

15,000 square miles (not including the Owyhee Range, which is closely related). Soils of the Idaho batholith are fragile and easily eroded. Land-disturbing activities such as logging, mining, and road and trail building result in rapid sedimentation of streams. The salmon run on the South Fork of the Salmon River fell by 90 percent from 1960 to 1976 because of destruction of spawning grounds and habitat due to erosion from new logging roads and also due to construction of new dams on the lower Snake and the Columbia rivers.

Mountain building did not end with the Mesozoic but continued into the Cenozoic era. In the early Tertiary Period new batholiths composed of pink granite were emplaced in areas of the Sawtooth Mountains and the Middle Fork of the Salmon River. At about the same time the Challis volcanics, which cover large areas from the Salmon River south towards Sun Valley, were extruded. This period also saw extensive block faulting that produced the Lost River, Sawtooth, and Pioneer mountains, and major downwarping that produced the Snake River Plain.

Beginning in the Miocene, basalt and rhyolite flows covered much of southern and western Idaho. The Columbia River basalts reached Weiser and Riggins. Rhyolite flows occurred in the Owyhee and Jarbidge mountains. In Quaternary times the Snake River basalt flows began to fill the Snake River Plain. This phase of volcanism is best observed at Craters of the Moon National Monument. The most recent phase of Idaho geologic history is the age of glaciation. Much of central Idaho has been altered by glacial action, and Idaho may still have one living glacier near Borah Peak.

Month	Mean High Temp.	Record High Temp.	Mean Low Temp.	Record Low Temp.	Total Precip. (Inches)	No. Days Greater Than 1/10″	No. Days Greater Than ½″
			OBSIDIAN — 6,900′				
May	57	79	27	6	1.3	4	+
June	65	91	31	14	1.2	3	+
July	77	95	35	18	.6	2	0
Aug.	76	93	33	10	.6	1	+
Sep.	68	89	27	−1	.8	2	+
Oct.	56	84	21	−12	1.0	1	0
			SUN VALLEY — 5,821′				
May	63	86	29	5	1.7	6	1
June	71	93	33	17	1.3	4	1
July	82	96	37	19	.7	2	+
Aug.	81	95	35	16	.6	1	+
Sep.	73	93	28	11	.7	2	+
Oct.	61	80	22	−3	1.1	3	1
			THREE CREEK — 5,410′				
Mar.	47	70	20	−14	1.2	4	+
Apr.	59	83	26	8	1.4	4	+
May	66	90	32	12	2.2	7	1
June	74	98	37	18	1.5	4	1
July	87	103	42	22	.4	1	+
Aug.	86	103	38	18	1.4	1	+
Sep.	77	99	31	8	1.7	2	+
Oct.	64	88	25	1	1.1	3	+

Flora and Fauna

Not surprisingly, plants are found in all parts of southern Idaho. The dominant tree in the mountains is the Douglas fir. Ponderosa, lodgepole, and whitebark pine are widespread, as are aspen, Engelmann spruce, and subalpine fir. Sagebrush, which dominates much of the desert, is also found in dry parts of the mountains. Wild flowers are undoubtedly one of the most enticing features of the mountain and desert world. Because of the 7,000-foot range of elevation in the area, flowers can be enjoyed from March to September. There are several nature trails in southern Idaho that can familiarize you with the area's plant life. Boise National Forest has the Mores Mountain Nature Trail north of Boise. The Payette National Forest has a new nature trail at Sheep Rock, near Cuprum, that overlooks Hell's Canyon. The Sawtooth National Recreation Area has a nature trail at the Redfish Lake Visitor Center and offers ranger-led hikes and campfire talks in the Sawtooth and Wood River valleys. Craters of the Moon National Monument and Bruneau Sand Dunes State Park each have desert-oriented nature trails.

Southern Idaho is home to a great variety of wildlife. The larger mammals are elk, mule deer, mountain goat, bighorn sheep, cougar, black bear, coyote, white-tailed deer, bobcat, and lynx. Smaller mammals include squirrels, chipmunk, marten, weasel, otter, badger, beaver, and porcupine. Frogs are common in mountain lakes and ponds, and toads are often seen roaming the forests. Lizards and snakes are frequently seen in lower elevations. The rattlesnake is rarely found above 5,000 feet. Bird lists are available from the Big Creek Ranger District (Payette National Forest) and the Sawtooth National Recreation Area.

HOW TO USE THIS BOOK

The remainder of this book describes fifty-four hikes in south-central and southwestern Idaho. These trips were selected on the basis of ease of access, wilderness character, scenic beauty, possibility of loop routes or extended trips, and a desire to introduce the reader to many different areas. The major features of the trip descriptions are: a list of key facts, including distances, difficulty of travel, seasons of use, and available maps; an overview of the hike and the area it is in; the trail description; ideas for extending weekend trips into longer ones; and directions for finding trailheads.

You are first given a simple system for describing the types of hikes that are possible in the area. "D" means a day hike in the four-to-nine-mile range. "O" means an overnight hike in the four-to-ten-mile range. Such a hike might start in midafternoon and finish at about the same time the next day. "W" indicates a two-night, weekend trip, and the trip descriptions are primarily oriented to such hikes. The weekend hikes are in the twelve-to-twenty-one-mile range. Such a hike might start Friday night with a short hike to a close-to-the-road campsite or early Saturday morning after camping at or near the trailhead. "L" indicates that longer trips, from three days to three weeks, can be planned. While the majority of these trips are suitable to all four types of hikes, it is important that you know (for instance) that there is no good day-hiker's goal or no acceptable overnighter's campsite on the hike.

The next key fact given is the total distance. Generally this figure is for the weekend hike; occasionally it is given for the overnight or day hike.

Next comes a classification of the hike according to three levels of difficulty. Level I hikes are suitable for beginners. They generally follow level terrain and use excellent, easy-to-follow trails. Level II hikes are for people of intermediate abililty. They are steeper than Level I hikes and may present route-finding problems. Level III trips require expert hiking skills. They usually have stretches of trail that are not only steep but also rocky, and they are often hard to follow. Some Level III hikes don't follow established trails at all but involve arduous cross-country travel where route-finding decisions must be made constantly. Many of the hikes start at a low level of difficulty but become tougher as they go along. Such hikes are noted as being of Levels I, II or Levels II, III.

The dates given for the seasons of use are necessarily estimates and may be off by two to three weeks. The starting dates are subject to the greatest variations, since every snow year and every thaw is different. You must check with forest headquarters or ranger stations for up-to-date information on roads and trails. The ending dates are either the usual opening day of the hunting season or October 1, whichever comes first. Backpacking is no fun when the bullets are flying, and travel in October runs the risk of severe weather. Remember that the dates are rough estimates. The reader who treats them as gospel will be disappointed from time to time.

United States Geological Survey (USGS) maps are essential tools for enjoying the outdoors. The USGS at last has good topographic map coverage of Idaho's backcountry. For many years remote areas were covered only by 1:250,000-scale maps originally surveyed by the Army Map Service. These were barely adequate for hiking and useful only in conjunction with a good Forest Service map. The last fifteen years, though, have seen a whole series of new 1:24,000-scale maps, and soon most of Idaho will be covered by these ultra-accurate maps. Many areas are still covered by 1:62,5000-scale maps, which the author prefers. Their inch-to-a-mile scale permits one map to cover most weekend trips. In contrast, the 1:24,000-scale maps show so much detail at two-and-a-half inches to a mile that they take some of the challenge out of hiking, and often several must be purchased to cover one trip. All USGS maps listed are assumed to be 1:24,000 scale unless otherwise noted. The maps followed by an asterisk (*) cover only small parts of the hike and are not absolutely necessary.

USGS maps are least expensive when ordered directly from the government. If you buy them locally you will usually pay a twenty-five cent premium. This quarter may be well spent, since ordering from Geological Survey map indexes can leave you with terrific maps of low-value territory, while local vendors let you preview maps before you buy. The problem of mail ordering maps you have not seen can be avoided by using public map repositories. These map reference libraries are located at Boise State University, the University of Idaho (Moscow), Idaho State University (Pocatello), and Ricks College (Rexberg). They have *all* maps for the entire United States, and can be used to preview hikes and maps inside and outside Idaho. When you request a state map index from the USGS (their address is in Appendix A), you will find on it a list of retail stores that sell the maps locally.

Just as USGS map availability is improving, so is the outlook for United States Forest Service (USFS) and Bureau of Land Management (BLM) maps. Forest boundary changes and forest road closures are being reflected in a new series of maps. Boise, Challis, and Sawtooth forest maps are now reasonably up-to-date, while new Payette National Forest (N.F.) maps are due in the early 1980s. You should purchase forest maps in the highly detailed Class C series — don't waste your money on the tourist-oriented Class F maps unless you are desperate. Your best sources for USFS maps are of course the national forest headquarters in Boise, McCall, Twin Falls, and Challis. Sawtooth National Recreation Area (N.R.A.) offices

near Ketchum and Stanley also carry forest maps. Addresses for these sources are given in Appendix A. District ranger stations usually have a few maps available.

You have three possible sources for maps of desert areas. The BLM is now producing excellent maps in a 1:100,000 scale. These show contours, land ownership, and major and minor roads. Big Sky, Metzgers, and other firms market county maps that show all the roads, good and bad, but don't give contours. The USGS now has good coverage of desert areas with 1:24,000-scale maps.

The maps in this book are hybrids, useful in planning hikes but of limited value in the field. They are based on Forest Service maps that are upgraded with critical elevations taken from USGS maps and updated with new roads, trails, and routes. Each map is drawn to an inch-to-a-mile scale and is based on a one inch, one mile grid. Most maps are oriented with north to the top, except for some full page maps which have north to the left. The symbols used in maps are:

Route:	••••••••••
Trail:	– – – – –
Poor dirt road:	⌶––⌶––⌶––⌶
Good dirt road:	⫞⫟⫟⫟⫟⫟⫟⫟⫟
Paved road:	▬ ▬ ▬ —
Stream:	〜
River:	〜〜
Major summit:	☼
Lake or pond:	⬤
Point with elevation:	x 6827
One mile:	├────────┤

Road mileage figures are given from Boise, the population and transportation center of the area. Trips toward McCall give directions and mileages from Scenic Junction, the intersection of Idaho Highway 44 (ID-44) and ID-55, six miles out State Street from Boise. Trips toward Idaho City, Lowman, and Stanley give directions from the Boise National Forest ranger station five miles east of Boise on ID-21 (Warm Springs Avenue). Trips toward Fairfield, Sun Valley, and Twin Falls give mileages from the intersection of Interstate 84 (I-84) and Broadway Avenue (Exit 54). Trips to the lower Snake River country give directions from I-84 and Meridian Road (Exit 44). The first mileage figure is the total miles to the trailhead. The second figure (in parentheses) is the amount of dirt road included in the total mileage.

The trail descriptions were field checked in 1978 and 1979. They should remain reasonably accurate for years, barring floods, slides, fires, or other catastrophes that can knock out bridges or trails. An effort has been made to identify campsites close to the trailhead, along the trail, and at the destination. This gives overnight campers more choices and weekend hikers more flexibility. Most of the ideas for extended trips are based on study of maps and land-use plans and not on personal experience. Any longer trip would require homework of your own, and you would want to contact the Forest Service or BLM for information on trail conditions.

Hopefully, you will never get lost on an Idaho forest or desert road. You probably will, though, in spite of the directions in this book. Mileages are approximate, because those given in the Access section are rounded off to half and quarter miles and because automobile odometers vary in accuracy. You should not immediately start to worry if a turnoff does not appear

exactly where it ought to. It will be right around the corner! Be sure to refer to your USGS and USFS maps before each hike.

Most of the drives in this book follow some dirt road, and dirt roads vary in quality. You may be lucky and use a road a week or two after it has received its annual grading. Or you may be unlucky and find it a muddy, rutted, bottomless pit. Under normal conditions almost all the access roads to hikes are open to full-size passenger cars. However, a pickup truck, which has the clearance to go over bumps, or a smaller car, which has the maneuverability to avoid them, is a better vehicle for dirt road driving. You should carry in your car a shovel, axe, and bucket. These are required for travel on some forest roads during high fire danger and are handy to have anytime. A "come-along" type winch with at least fifty feet of cable can be helpful if you get stuck in mud, snow, or water.

Idaho's roads are among the most dangerous in the nation. Certain roads at certain times may be among the most hazardous anywhere (such as Idaho 21 from Idaho City to Boise at 1 A.M. on weekends). You can increase your chances of survival on dirt roads by honking your horn on blind turns in daylight. Some dirt roads may be safer to drive at night, when you can see the headlights of oncoming cars. But at night you must be more wary of animals, for there are some five hundred collisions with animals on Idaho roads each year. Perhaps the best precaution you can take on Idaho highways and byways is a lucky rabbit's foot. Good luck!

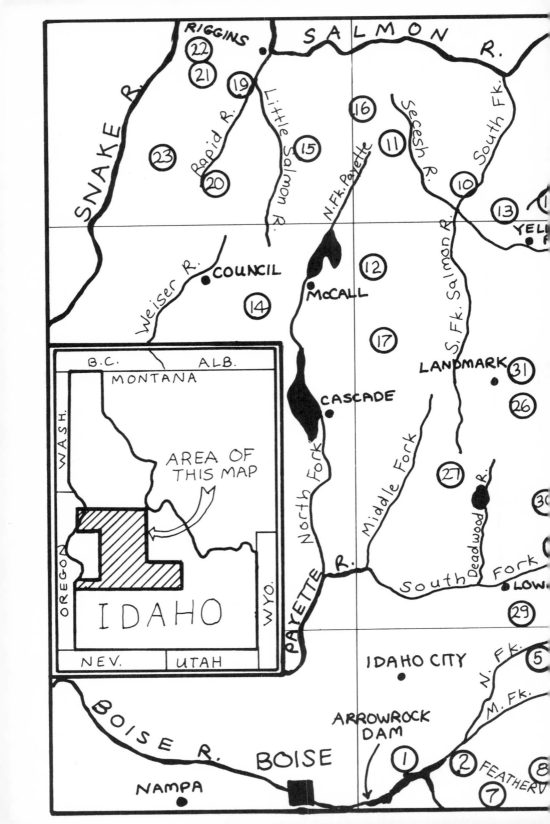

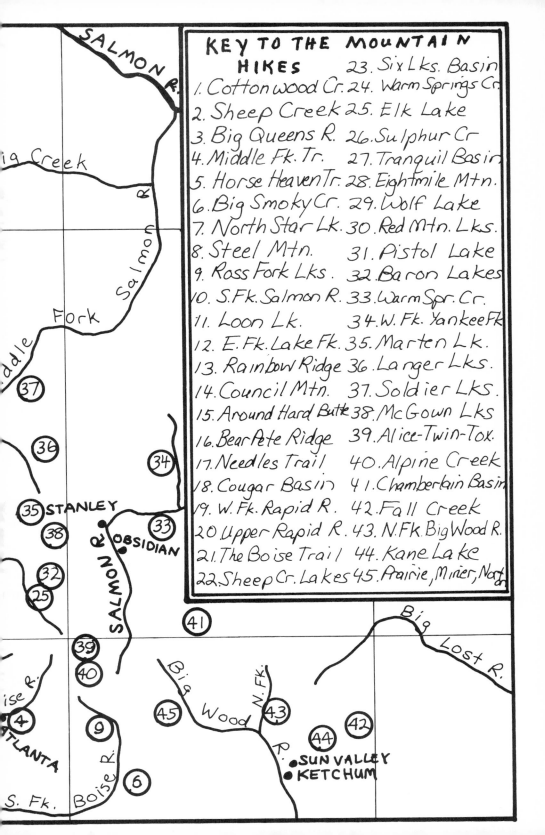

KEY TO THE MOUNTAIN HIKES

1. Cottonwood Cr.
2. Sheep Creek
3. Big Queens R.
4. Middle Fk. Tr.
5. Horse Heaven Tr.
6. Big Smoky Cr.
7. North Star Lk.
8. Steel Mtn.
9. Ross Fork Lks.
10. S.Fk. Salmon R.
11. Loon Lk.
12. E.Fk. Lake Fk.
13. Rainbow Ridge
14. Council Mtn.
15. Around Hard Butte
16. Bear Pete Ridge
17. Needles Trail
18. Cougar Basin
19. W.Fk. Rapid R.
20. Upper Rapid R.
21. The Boise Trail
22. Sheep Cr. Lakes
23. Six Lks. Basin
24. Warm Springs Cr.
25. Elk Lake
26. Sulphur Cr
27. Tranquil Basin
28. Eightmile Mtn.
29. Wolf Lake
30. Red Mtn. Lks.
31. Pistol Lake
32. Baron Lakes
33. Warm Spr. Cr.
34. W. Fk. Yankee Fk.
35. Marten Lk.
36. Langer Lks.
37. Soldier Lks.
38. McGown Lks
39. Alice-Twin-Tox.
40. Alpine Creek
41. Chamberlain Basin
42. Fall Creek
43. N.Fk. Big Wood R.
44. Kane Lake
45. Prairie, Miner, North

Area One

FORKS OF THE BOISE RIVER

The Boise River is Boise's river. From its sources in high mountain lakes to its impoundments behind lowland reservoirs, the Boise's creeks, meadows, and mountains offer great hiking and camping to the people who live in its valley. These hikes can be made in sequence from lowest to highest as the season unfolds, from Cottonwood and Sheep Creeks in early spring to the Ross Fork and Spangle Lakes in high summer. Most of these are fairly easy streamside hikes that offer excellent camping.

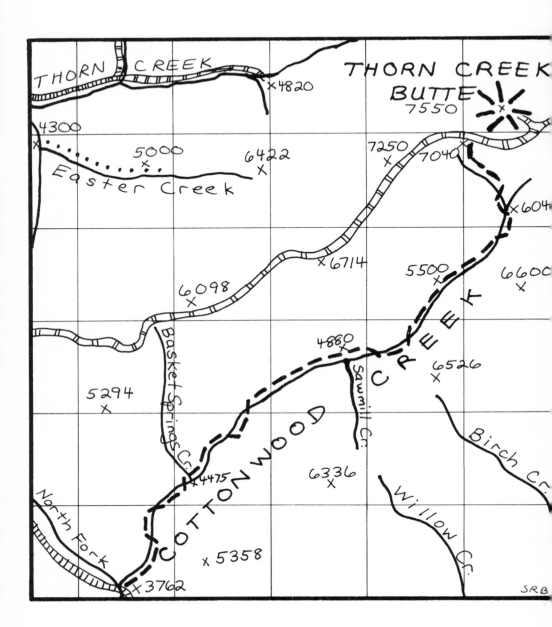

THORN CREEK

THORN CREEK BUTTE
7550 ×

×4820

4300
×

5000
×

6422
×

7250
×

7040

×604

Easter Creek

×6714

5500
×

6600
×

6098
×

Basket Springs Cr.

4880
×

C R E E K

6526
×

5294
×

Sawmill Cr.

COTTONWOOD

Birch Cr.

×4475

6336
×

Willow Cr.

North Fork

×5358

×3762

SRB

COTTONWOOD CREEK

HIKES: D, O, W.
TOTAL DISTANCE, W: 11 Miles.
DIFFICULTY: Level I.
SEASON: March 15 — October 1.
USGS MAP: Arrowrock Reservoir NE.
USFS MAP: Boise N.F.
MILEAGE: 30½ (17 Dirt).

INTRODUCTION: The upper Cottonwood Creek drainage is the closest roadless area to Boise. It provides excellent early season hiking. The area was logged years ago, and at times the trail uses the old logging road. Though the trail is easy to follow and in good condition, it lacks bridges for the numerous stream crossings. It is suitable for Level I hikers who aren't afraid to get their feet wet or who are willing to wait until June when the stream goes down. Such lower elevation hikes in the Boise drainage are in rattlesnake country, so keep your eyes open.

THE TRAIL: Your goal is the old sawmill site by Sawmill Creek, 5½ miles in. Day-hikers may stop at Basket Springs Creek, 3 miles in, and overnight campsites start 2 miles from the road. The trail begins at the Bald Mountain Trail sign. Climb to the left to reach the old road. Just before the first crossing, a solid mile in, are a few campsites. More good sites lie between the second and third crossings. After the fifth crossing a good hike takes you to the old mill site, where there is a large clearing. More good campsites are along the trail between the mill site and the sixth crossing, and across the creek from there. For your return hike you might try to climb up to the ridge south of Cottonwood Creek and follow it back to the road. A primitive trail follows the ridgeline.

EXTENSIONS: The trail reaches Bald Mountain (Thorn Creek Butte) after several more miles, stream crossings, and climbing stretches. There are campsites along the creek below 6,210 and at the East Fork junction. The upper trailhead, eight miles from the North Fork Cottonwood Creek — Thorn Creek summit by a rough road, is signed, and there are campsites along the trail before it makes its plunge.

ACCESS: Drive 11 miles past the Boise N.F. ranger station on ID-21 and turn right on the Middle Fork Boise River Road. Cautiously drive 16½ miles, past Arrowrock Dam, and turn left on Cottonwood Creek Road. The trailhead is 2½ miles up the road, just before the bridge over the creek. There is a good campground downstream from the ranger station, a few campsites near the trailhead, and camping 2 miles up the trail. A new cabin area near the trailhead may obscure the very start of your route. Check with the Boise N.F. for possible changes.

Springtime hiking at its best — Cottonwood Creek

SHEEP CREEK

HIKES: D, O, W, L.
TOTAL DISTANCE, W: 15 Miles.
DIFFICULTY: Level II.
SEASON: April 1 — October 1.
USGS MAPS: Twin Springs, Sheep Creek.
USFS MAP: Boise N.F.
MILEAGE: 41½ (29 Dirt).

INTRODUCTION: Sheep Creek drains a large roadless area near Boise that has much to offer any hiker: early season hiking, a wide range of elevations, good trails, trailless areas, historical sites, and a chance for long trips. The first eight miles of the main Sheep Creek Trail are generally level and easy to follow, making this hike Level II. Snakes are here!

THE TRAIL: Your goal is the forks of Sheep Creek, 8 miles in. Day-hikers may go to the first crossing, 3 miles in, while overnighters may go to either the South Fork (2½ miles) or to Devil's Creek (5 miles). The trail starts by lazily switching back to the level of an old mining flume, where it divides. Go left, and follow the flume for a mile. When the main trail descends from the flume level to cross a drainage, a poor trail goes down to the South Fork and some campsites. The main trail climbs again and stays high until it comes to the bridge at the first crossing of Sheep Creek.

Crossing the creek takes you from a dry southern exposure to a wet northern exposure, and you enter a new world of lush vegetation and frequent creeks. The next campsites are near the second crossing, which has a crossing log upstream. The trail stays on the north side of the creek until it reaches the confluence of the East Fork and the main Sheep Creek, where there are campsites.

EXTENSIONS: A fine loop trip would be to hike on to the Trinities via either the East Fork or main Sheep Creek and return via Devil's Creek. Other interesting trails in the area lead up Devil's Creek and over to Corral Creek (past some old cabins). And finally, the South Fork Sheep Creek has no trails and offers high-challenge hiking.

ACCESS: Go 11 miles past the Boise N.F. ranger station on ID-21 and turn right on the Middle Fork Boise River Road. After 30 miles you cross the river for the first time. Just past this bridge is the trailhead. There is no camping at the trailhead or during the first 2 miles, but there are several Forest Service campgrounds along the Middle Fork Road before and after the trailhead.

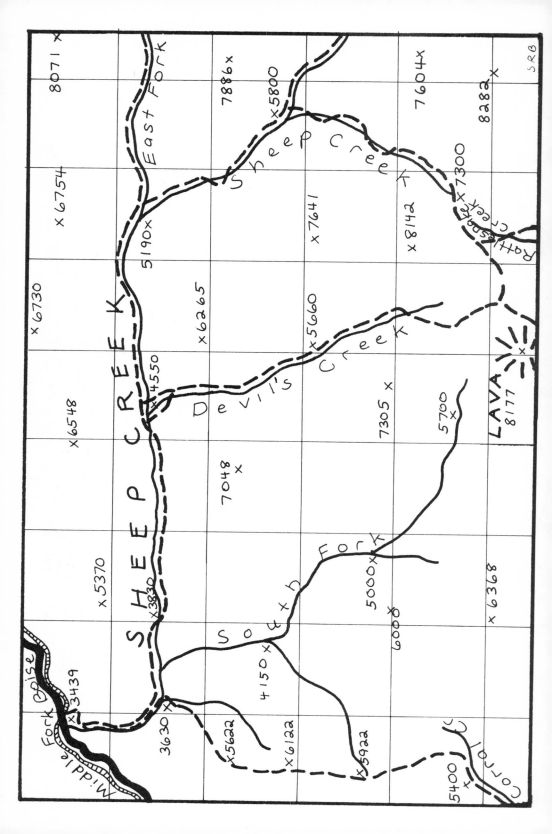

An old mining flume above the Sheep Creek Trail

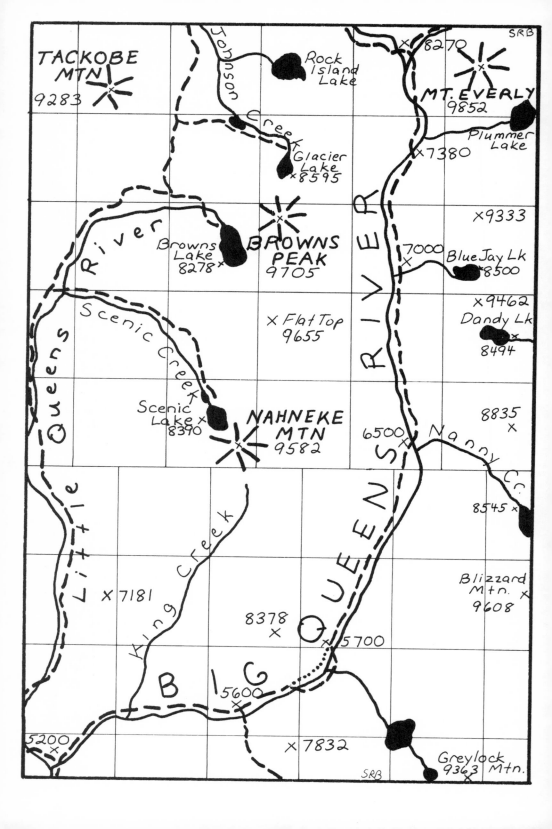

BIG QUEENS RIVER

HIKES: D, O, W, L.
TOTAL DISTANCE, W: 16 Miles.
DIFFICULTY: Levels I, II.
SEASON: May 20 — October 1.
USGS MAPS: Atlanta East*, Atlanta West, Mt. Everly.
USFS MAP: Boise N.F. or Sawtooth Wilderness Area (Sawtooth N.R.A.).
MILEAGE: 76½ (63½ Dirt).

INTRODUCTION: This magnificent trail in the southern Sawtooths starts at only 5,200 feet and has an excellent southern exposure. It is not only an exciting place for early season hiking but a great gateway for later season exploration of a little-used part of the Sawtooths. The first 3½ miles of trail are flat and easy to follow, Level I. When the canyon closes in, the stream crossings and climbing stretches make the hike Level II.

THE TRAIL: Your goal is the third crossing of Queens River, 8 miles in. Overnighters and day-hikers will stop at the first crossing, 3½ miles in. Begin by crossing the river on the old bridge and turning right. The first miles are on an old road that wanders through meadows and ponderosa pine and gives an ever-improving view. Gradually the canyon narrows, the road disappears, and the yellow pine is replaced by lodgepole. Several creeks cross your route, and you may camp by them or by the river. After you pass the Joe Daley Trail junction, you begin to notice the pink rock of the Sawtooth batholith at your feet. There are a few campsites near the first crossing, a ford that can be dangerous at high water.

The crossing and the one that follows it can be avoided. A decent route stays on the left bank for the ½ mile to the next crossing. To find it, go upstream to a rockslide and stay near its base until it ends. Then climb the stream bank, and you should intersect a poor trail that meets the main trail just above the second crossing.

The trail climbs between the second and third crossings, passing very few campsites. In early season it enters a spectacular world of snowfields and waterfalls. You may encounter a vast snow bridge spanning the river, whose waters, when viewed from above, may look as white as the snow the feeds them. The third crossing is easier than the first two, and there is camping across the river.

EXTENSIONS: Many outstanding longer hikes are possible. Queens River becomes more beautiful the farther up you hike. Lush meadows and attractive campsites are the rule. An excellent loop goes up Big Queens and down Little Queens River. Pats Lake, along the way, can be used as a base for climbing to views of some of the Sawtooths' most rugged and remote peaks, including North Raker. Another loop can be made via Rock Creek or Benedict Creek to the Middle Fork Boise River and then back by way of Atlanta and the difficult Joe Daley Trail. Or you may just keep hiking north, to exit at Grandjean, Hell Roaring Lake, or the Iron Creek Campground.

ACCESS: Follow directions to Atlanta (see the Middle Fork Trail, page 37) as far as Swanholm Junction. Go 10 miles farther and take a left at the Queens River Road. The trailhead is 2½ miles in, on an often rough road. There is good camping at the trailhead, at established Forest Service campgrounds on the Middle Fork, or a very short distance down the trail.

Queen's River foothills — Big Queen's River

THE MIDDLE FORK TRAIL

HIKES: D, O, W, L.
TOTAL DISTANCE, W: 13 Miles.
DIFFICULTY: Level I.
SEASON: June 5 — October 1.
USGS MAP: Atlanta East
USFS MAP: Boise N.F. or Sawtooth Wilderness Area (Sawtooth N.R.A.).
MILEAGE: 83 (70 Dirt).

INTRODUCTION: Atlanta, one of Idaho's most remote communities, sits at the end of the road and the start of the trails. The best trail out of Atlanta is the Middle Fork Boise River Trail, a Sawtooth-style "mountain highway" that leads to the popular Spangle Lakes. It is built and maintained to the highest standards and is well suited to Level I hikers.

THE TRAIL: Your goal is Mattingly Creek, 6½ miles in. Overnighters may camp near Leggit Creek, 3 miles in, while day-hikers should walk the extra ½ mile to the view at 6,050. After the trail leaves the campground it passes good campsites all the way to Leggit Creek. Beyond the creek the trail climbs in long, lazy switchbacks. The Leggit Lake Trail, rugged and steep, leaves from the top of the climb at 6,050. When you come to the open area by Corral Creek the trail divides. Bear left and you will soon see campsites. There are more sites across Mattingly Creek.

Several good day hikes may be taken from a base camp here. Good views of super-rugged Mattingly Peak can be had by going up Mattingly Creek or the Middle Fork. Hiking to the Lynx Creek Lakes would doubtless be tough but rewarding.

EXTENSIONS: The whole world of the southern Sawtooths is open to you from here. Up the Middle Fork are the Rock Creek Trail (4 more miles), the Flytrip Creek Trail (7 miles), and the Spangle Lakes (10 miles). Alturas Lake is 10 miles away by way of Mattingly Creek.

ACCESS: There are two main routes to Atlanta. One leads all the way up the Middle Fork Boise River Road, turning right 11 miles past the Boise N.F. ranger station and then following the river for 72 miles to Atlanta. Once you enter town, follow signs for the Power Plant Recreation Area, taking a right-left to the stop sign by the bars. Go straight and then bear left at the Talache Mine Road. The trailhead, on the right at the edge of a meadow, is well marked. There is a large campground here and lots of camping just down the trail. You can also reach Atlanta by way of Idaho City, using the Crooked River Road, the North Fork Boise River Road, and the Swanholm Creek Road to reach the Middle Fork at Swanholm Junction, where you turn left for Atlanta.

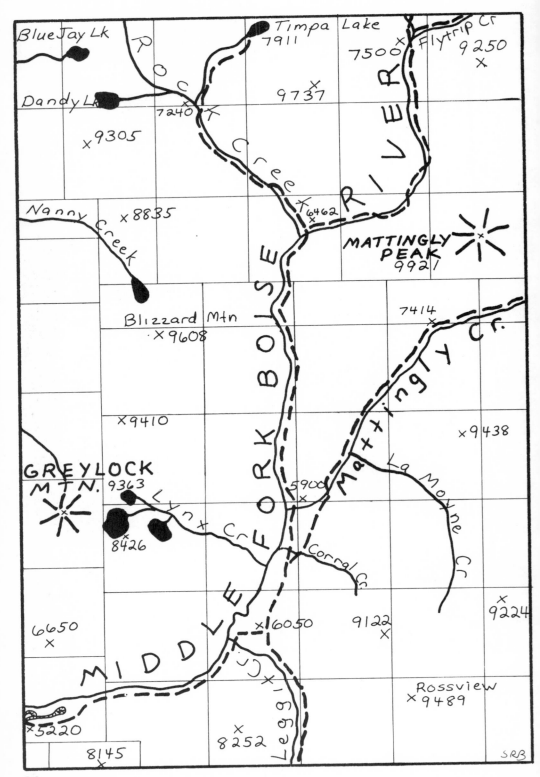

BlueJay Lk

Timpa Lake
7911

Flytrip Cr
9250
X

7500
X

Dandy Lk

ROCK

9737
X

7240 X

×9305

Creek

×8835

×6462
X

MATTINGLY
PEAK
9921
×

Nanny Creek

BOISE RIVER

7414
×

Blizzard Mtn
×9608

Mattingly Cr.

×9410

×9438

GREYLOCK
M̄T̄N. 9363

Lynx Cr

5900
×

La Moyne Cr

×
8426

Corral Cr

×9224

6650
×

×6050

9122
×

MIDDLE FORK

Leggit Cr

Rossview
×9489

×5220

8252
×

8145
×

SRB

38

Down by the riverside — Middle Fork of Boise River

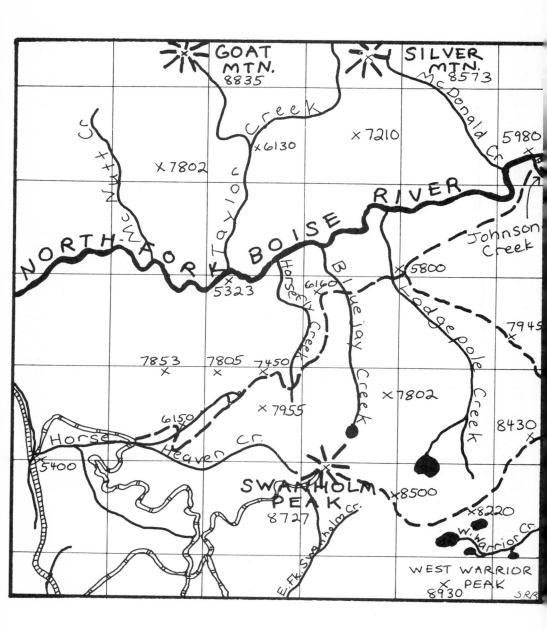

HORSE HEAVEN TRAIL

HIKES: D, O, W, L.
TOTAL DISTANCE, W: 15 Miles.
DIFFICULTY: Level II.
SEASON: June 10 — October 1.
USGS MAP: Swanholm Peak.
USFS MAP: Boise N.F.
MILEAGE: 70½ (35½ Dirt).

INTRODUCTION: A large roadless area lies to the west of the Sawtooth Wilderness Area. It stretches from the Middle Fork Boise River to the South Fork Payette River. It includes the Swanholm-West Warrior area, a 10-mile stretch of the North Fork Boise River, the Wolf Mountain-Goat Mountain area, and the Tyee Mountain-Tenmile Mountain region. Only one road, that to Graham Guard Station, penetrates the area, and it opens late, closes early, and is poorly maintained. This Tenmile Wilderness received a "further planning" decision from RARE II. If Idaho hikers want to preserve it, they must fight for it. There are few trails in the region, the best one being the Horse Heaven Trail from Horse Heaven Creek to Johnson Creek. This trail has some steep stretches but is generally easy to follow, so it is Level II.

THE TRAIL: Your goal is Johnson Creek, 7½ miles in. Day-hikers and overnighters may hike to the divide or the cabin site below it, 3 miles in. The trail starts on a not-so-old logging road which is already severely eroded. There are a few dry campsites after the road's initial climb from Horse Heaven Creek. As you walk on the road you can see Swanholm Lookout high above you. The trail bears off the road to the left just where the USGS map

shows — before the second crossing of Horse Heaven Creek (at a small bridge). Climb along the left side of the creek, cross it, and then climb to the right until you round a corner and confront Steel Mountain. The springs shown on the map should provide water right on the trail. Just beyond the springs are the remains of a small cabin. You may camp by the cabin or on the saddle past it.

You should stop at the saddle and gawk. Across the North Fork is the Wolf-Goat area, a land without trails. After a bit more hiking you can see many Sawtooth peaks, including distinctive North Raker. The trail descends quickly after crossing Horsefly Creek and then contours to a ridge above Blue Jay Creek. It rapidly loses more altitude to the crossing of Blue Jay, which must be forded in early season. Lodgepole Creek, not far beyond, has a crossing log downstream. The trail from Lodgepole Creek to Johnson Creek is a gentle one. It passes through a lodgepole forest that offers abundant dry camps near the trail and countless wet ones along the river. Civilization, in the form of a USFS campground, lies just across Johnson Creek.

EXTENSIONS: A good loop is possible in this area. It cuts right off the trail at the high saddle, follows a poor trail up to Swanholm Peak, hikes past the Warrior Lakes, and descends the Lodgepole Trail to the Horse Heaven Trail. The North Fork Boise River Trail, which shows on Forest Service maps, has many washed-out stretches.

ACCESS: There are two routes. The early season route leaves ID-21 35 miles past the Boise N.F. ranger station, turning right on the Rabbit Creek Road. It follows this road to the North Fork Boise River and then follows the North Fork Road to the Deer Park Bridge. There, just before Deer Park Guard Station, it crosses the river and continues 1¾ miles to the unsigned trailhead, where the logging road crosses Horse Heaven Creek in a clearing to the left. A better route that opens later turns right off ID-21, 50 miles past the ranger station at the Crooked River Road. It follows signs for Atlanta, turning left on the North Fork Boise River Road to reach the Deer Park Bridge. Both the Rabbit Creek and Crooked River roads have heavy logging truck traffic, so be careful. There is camping in Forest Service campgrounds on the North Fork and also on the logging road just past the trailhead.

Rubber boa on patrol at Horse Heaven Trail

BIG SMOKY CREEK

HIKES: D, O, W, L.
TOTAL DISTANCE, W: 16 Miles.
DIFFICULTY: Levels I, III.
SEASON: June 1 — October 1.
USGS MAP: Paradise Peak.
USFS MAP: Fairfield Ranger District (Sawtooth N.F.).
MILEAGE: 128 (16 Dirt).

INTRODUCTION: Big Smoky Creek is as big as a river, and it drains a large and beautiful roadless area that stretches from the Smoky Mountains west of Sun Valley to the most southern Sawtooths near Vienna. The RARE II study did not include lower Big Smoky Creek in the proposed South Boise Wilderness. There are good campsites along the creek, which boasts an easygoing Level I trail. The area has an extensive trail system whose components are in various states of repair. A Level III loop route is possible using the benignly neglected Skillern Creek Trail.

THE TRAIL: Your goal is the North Fork Big Smoky Creek, 8 miles in. More advanced hikers may opt to return by the Skillern Creek Trail, a slightly longer route. Day-hikers and overnighters may stop at Skillern Hot Springs, 3 miles in.

During the first two miles of trail you pass many good campsites and then climb to cross Poison Creek and avoid a crossing of Big Smoky Creek. You then descend to the river again and pass some good campsites around Skillern Creek. The hot springs near the creek are in a completely natural condition and should stay that way! As you continue along the trail you will see Big Peak Creek on the other side of Big Smoky. Crossing here to reach the Big Peak Trail would mean a difficult ford

in any season. From here to the North Fork the trail makes two climbs, each of which is followed by a descent to a wide grassy bar offering unlimited camping.

A return via Skillern Creek requires Level III skills, as this route is very steep, very rough, and very hard to follow. Cross the North Fork Big Smoky and turn left on its trail. The Skillern Creek Trail, which is unsigned, crosses the North Fork well past Little Pinyon Creek, the first drainage on the left. Find the blazes on trees on both sides of the crossing and then seek a handy log downstream to cross on. Climb until you first come to water. Don't cross that fork of Little Pinyon — turn right and climb an open stretch that shows on the USGS map. The trail then cuts right, up a draw, switches left, crosses a dry stream bed, and again comes to the fork of Little Pinyon. Fill your canteen, cross, and climb! The Forest Service left out a few switchbacks on this stretch, where you may find snow in early season.

Once over the steep stretch you climb along the ridgeline with your pass at 7,878 feet in view. Just where the trail leaves the ridge to contour and climb to that pass is unclear, as the trail is rough and seems to divide. If you lose it while contouring, it is probably above you. Skillern Peak is an easy climb from the pass.

The trail descends to the right and crosses a tributary of Skillern Creek. After you cross, stay to the right of the creek at all times, regardless of what your maps say. There are campsites along the way to main Skillern Creek. After crossing the main creek the trail stays high on its west side. When it suddenly takes a right at a gully, you meet the Poison Creek Trail. This trail makes an easy climb and descent to that creek, where there are some campsites.

EXTENSIONS: Long loop hikes are possible in the Smokies. One loop would go up Big Smoky and Bluff Creeks to Baker Lake and return via Big Peak Creek. Another would go up the West Fork Big

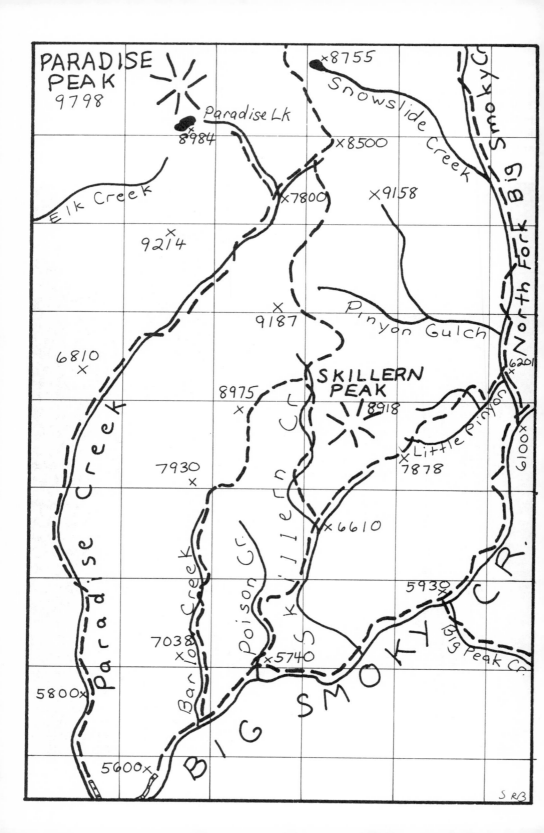

Smoky Creek to Snowslide Lakes and return via the Barlow Creek Trail.

ACCESS: Take I-84 from Broadway to Exit 95, US-20. Turn left and drive 60 miles to Fairfield, where you take another left. Stay on the paved road for 10 miles and then bear right on the Couch Summit-Big Smoky Road. After 9 more miles turn left on the Little Smoky Creek Road. After another 5½ miles cross the Big Smoky Bridge and turn right to the Canyon Campground, your trailhead. You may camp there or along the river beside the trail.

Big Smoky Creek is as big as a river.

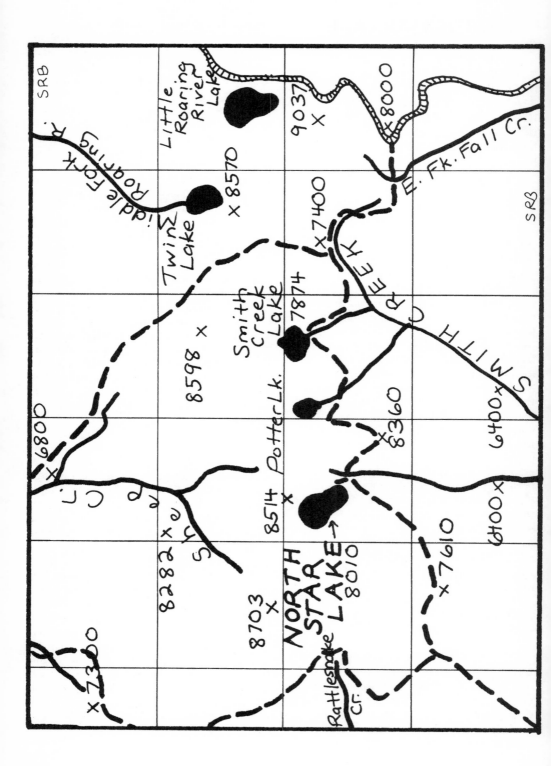

46

NORTH STAR LAKE

HIKES: D, O, W, L.
TOTAL DISTANCE, W: 12 Miles.
DIFFICULTY: Level III.
SEASON: July 4 — October 1.
USGS MAPS: Trinity Mountain, Prairie*.
USFS MAP: Boise N.F.
MILEAGE: 90½ (28 Dirt).

INTRODUCTION: The Trinity Mountains form a beautiful island in the sky, towering high above the South Fork Boise River. A road bisects the Trinities into a small, steep, roadless area with several lakes to the east, and a larger, more open roadless area with fewer lakes to the west. North Star Lake is in the western section. It is the farthest Trinities lake from the road and the closest (as the crow flies) mountain lake to Boise. Forest Service neglect of this trail prompted some citizen to take matters — specifically, a can of orange spray paint — into his own hands to blaze the trail. The blazing job has been poorly done, but it makes the point that if the government doesn't care for its backcountry the people will, and that spray-paint blazes can be long-lasting and effective. (The Forest Service frowns on spray-painted blazes because of the obnoxious orange color. Why not try a nice mellow gold in the hue of fresh sap?) This is a Level III hike due to the steep, rocky, hard-to-follow trail.

THE TRAIL: Your goal is North Star Lake, 6 miles in. The day-hiker's or overnighter's goal can be either a trail divide on Smith Creek, 2 miles in, or Smith Creek Lake, 3 miles in. Start off on an old road, and after a short walk you will cross a picturesque little stream where the trail begins. You then descend to a saddle with some camping, where you turn right. Bear to the left of the creek as you descend, and then cross. Stay to its right until you come to a flat open area with campsites and a trail divide.

The trail to the right leads over the hill to Sheep Creek, but you want to go left towards Lava Mountain. Once you enter the Smith Creek Lake drainage stay to the right of its stream all the way to the lake, where you may camp. Cross the dam at the lake and take a trail that contours along to the Potter Lake drainage. This route is much better than the trail shown on the USFS map, which has been neglected. Your contouring trail meets the mapped trail just before it crosses Potter Lake Creek. After a short climb it abruptly cuts back to the left and starts a steep ascent to a magnificent viewpoint. From here you can see Smith Prairie, Danskin and Trinity lookouts, North Star Lake, and the Lava Mountain Trail. Here you are already 2,000 feet above Smith Creek. There are several campsites by North Star Lake, with more above it to the west. A good spring flows into its west-northwest corner.

EXTENSIONS: Good hikes can be made in the direction of Sheep Creek. A nice loop would go by Rattlesnake Mountain, Devils Creek, and main Sheep Creek to the Smith Creek Trail divide you passed earlier. An extra day would permit exploration of Lava Mountain or Rattlesnake Creek.

ACCESS: Take I-84 from Broadway to Exit 95. Go left on US-20 for 21 miles, and turn left on the Anderson Ranch Dam Road. Cross the dam, turn right, and go 9 miles to the Fall Creek Road junction. Turn left and follow this steep road for almost 19 miles to the trailhead at the western end of a switchback in the road. USFS campgrounds are just over the summit and 2 miles back down the road. A saddle, ½ mile in, offers limited camping on the trail.

North Star Lake — a near miss

STEEL MOUNTAIN

HIKES: D, O, W.
TOTAL DISTANCE, O: 4 Miles.
DIFFICULTY: Level III.
SEASON: July 4 — October 1.
USGS MAPS: Phifer Creek, Rocky Bar.
USFS MAP: Boise N.F.
MILEAGE: 117 (43 Dirt).

INTRODUCTION: Steel Mountain is a spectacular peak, its 9,730-foot summit dominating a vast area between the Middle and South Forks of the Boise River. It can easily be viewed from the Mores Mountain Nature Trail above Boise. A lack of maintained trails makes the area around the mountain highly challenging for Level III hikers.

THE TRAIL: The day-hiker's and overnighter's goal is a camping area at the east end of a large meadow, about 2 miles in. Weekenders may use this spot as a base for hikes up Steel Mountain or over to Lake Creek Lake. The trail starts at the point where the left side of the bulldozer gouge meets the road cut. Go directly up the bank and stay left of the drainage that leads up from the gouge. Once you are on the "trail" (a poor route infrequently blazed by sheepherders), you will find it fun to follow. It goes through brush, follows streams, crosses downed logs, and often leaves you breathless. At last the terrain levels out in a forest, and there are campsites. At the end of this forest (your goal) is a long meadow from which you can see Steel Mountain's two lower, eastern summits.

Past the campsite the trail becomes even fainter. It seems to cross Elk Creek right where the meadow begins and to stay left of the creek for a mile to another meadow. It then cuts south to climb to the 8,350-foot divide with Steel Creek, passing many springs along the way. The saddle is your jump-off point for climbing Steel Mountain. The old trail continues down Steel Creek toward Rocky Bar.

Lake Creek Lake is one of the Boise N.F.'s most remote. Several routes, all of which look difficult, suggest themselves to the east of, to the west of, and right over the top of the 8,889–8,952-foot ridge.

EXTENSIONS: You might go down Lake Creek from the lake to the trail that contours along Steel Mountain's northern flank and then go east to the James Creek Road.

ACCESS: Drive out I-84 from Broadway Avenue to US-20, Exit 95. Turn left and drive 32½ miles to the Pine exit (just across Cat Creek Summit). Turn left and drive to Featherville via Pine. Take a left at the Rocky Bar turnoff in Featherville. Continue 8 miles to that ghost town and turn right on the James Creek Road to Atlanta. As far as the trailhead the road is steep and rough but usually passable for sedans. (It gets much worse on the Atlanta side.) After a short ½ mile bear left, and after another ½ mile bear right. Three more miles bring you to Elk Creek. Drive 100 yards beyond the creek and park your car. The trail begins at a bulldozed cut in the hill to your left. There are no campsites near the trailhead, but you can camp at James Creek Summit 3 miles up the road.

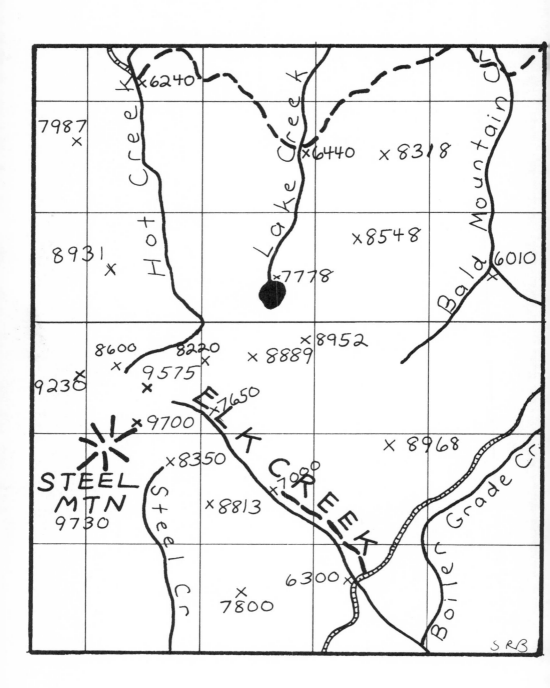

Steel Mountain, a magnificent monolith

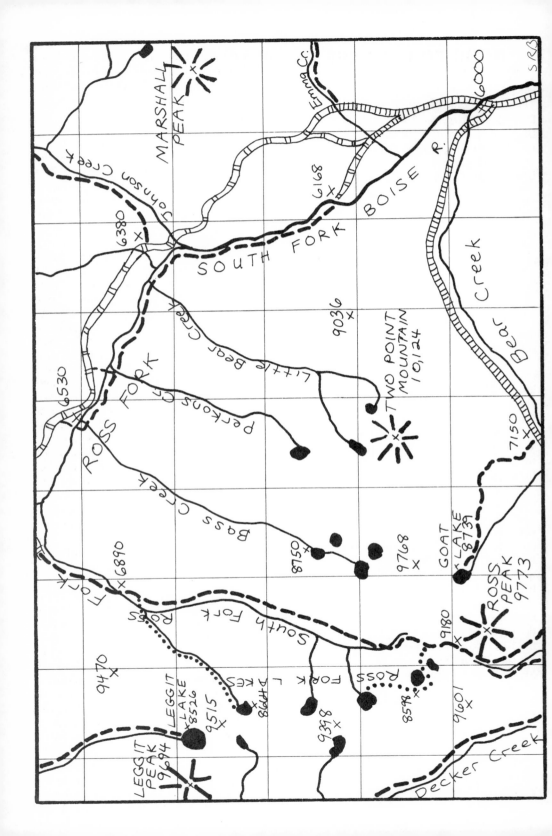

ROSS FORK LAKES

HIKES: D, O, W, L.
TOTAL DISTANCES, W: 24 Miles.
DIFFICULTY: Levels I, II, III.
SEASON: June 30 — October 1.
USGS MAPS: Marshall Park, Ross Peak, Atlanta East.
USFS MAP: Fairfield Ranger District (Sawtooth N.F.).
MILEAGE: 132½ (25 Dirt).

INTRODUCTION: The Boise River's South Fork is born where Ross Fork and Johnson Creek meet. The RARE II study endorsed the area drained by these two streams for wilderness classification. It is a land of broad valleys, steep mountains, and rugged trails, two of which lead to the four Ross Fork lakes. The Ross Fork Basin Trail starts off as easy Level I and ends up as strenuous Level III. An alternate trail from Bear Creek is steep, rocky Level III hiking all the way.

THE TRAILS: The Ross Fork Horse Trail is little used and little maintained, yet it is in good condition. It takes you to the Bass Creek Trail, which crosses Ross Fork and joins the Ross Fork Motor Trail, which leads to the South Fork Ross Fork trail, which leads to Ross Fork Lake No. 4, 12 miles in. Day-hikers and overnighters may hike up the Horse Trail and return down the Motor Trail, a 7-mile loop. If the South Fork Boise River is too high to ford on the Horse Trail, you can stay on the Motor Trail, a four-wheel-drive road that boasts a footbridge over Johnson Creek. There are many campsites along both trails in Ross Fork Basin.

Where the Motor Trail ends, the South Fork Ross Fork Trail begins. It moves from trees to meadows to trees, with avalanche-scarred slopes on either side.

After the first crossing, a sign points out a steep trail to Ross Fork Lake No. 1. More climbing on the main trail takes you to the second crossing. A large meadow on the other side offers camping.

Just past here The Big Climb begins, and you must gain 800 feet in ½ mile. At the climb's end you cross the creek that drains a big pond next to Lake No. 4. Turn right and follow the north end of the pond/marsh to reach the campsites above the lake. A rough trail leaves the west side of the lake and contours toward Lake No. 3.

A shorter (5 miles) but rougher route to Lake No. 4 leaves the Bear Creek Road. It then drops into the upper Willow Creek drainage and climbs to a beautiful pass just under Ross Peak and just above the lake. If your car can ford Goat Creek you can drive another 1¼ miles to the Bear Creek crossing, where the road becomes very steep. Hike up the road to a switchback at Red Horse Mine. The trail leaves the road here, passing behind an old cabin. It makes its way to a signed trail divide at the saddle between Bear and Willow creeks. Go right from here and descend towards Willow Creek. The junction with the Willow Creek Trail is not signed but seems to come just after you begin climbing. The marshy area shown on the USGS map makes good camping after it has dried out a bit. The view from the saddle extends north up South Fork Ross Fork to North Fork Ross Fork and on to the southern Sawtooths — superb! The descent to Lake No. 4 is very steep.

EXTENSIONS: One loop hike in the area would start on Bear Creek, go to Ross Lake No. 4, descend Ross Fork to Bass Creek, and return via the Bass Lakes and Goat Lake. Another loop would climb the North Fork Ross Fork (trail not signed) to Alturas Lake Creek and return via Johnson Creek. The Willow Creek Trail descends 10 miles to the South Fork Boise River.

ACCESS: Follow directions for Big Smoky Creek as far as the Big Smoky Bridge. Go straight here, climbing on the narrow, twisting South Fork Road. Follow the road past the Bear Creek Road, past the South Fork Campground, to the Emma Creek ford, 10½ miles in all. You may park there or cross if you can. The divide between the Motor Trail and the Horse Trail is ½ mile farther. There are campsites along the Horse Trail before and after its crossing of the South Fork.

Looking north to the Sawtooths from Ross Fork

Area Two
AROUND McCALL

McCall marks the western edge of the Salmon River Range. The topography near this town ranges from the sheer granite slopes of Jughandle Peak to the majestic gorge of the South Fork Salmon River, from the glacial carved, lake-studded valley of Lick Creek to the forested expanses of French Creek. While most of the roadless areas around McCall have been slated for development, the mountains on both sides of Lick Creek have been endorsed for wilderness by the Forest Service's RARE II study. McCall also serves as a jump-off point for long hikes in the River of No Return Wilderness Area.

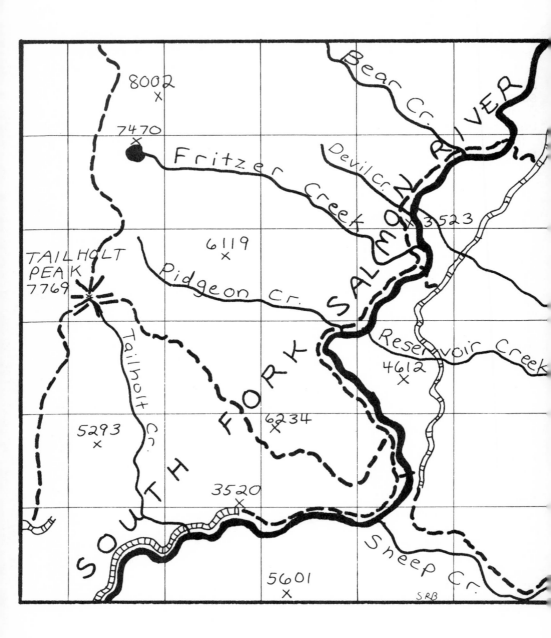

SOUTH FORK SALMON RIVER

HIKES: D, O, L.
TOTAL DISTANCE, O: 11 Miles.
DIFFICULTY: Level I.
SEASON: May 1 — September 25.
USGS MAP: Williams Peak.
USFS MAP: Krassel Ranger District (Payette N.F.).
MILEAGE: 136 (34 Dirt).

INTRODUCTION: The South Fork Salmon River rises south of Warm Lake and is paralleled by a road for much of its course. Along one stretch, though, the river cuts a canyon that the road can't conquer. Hiking the trail through this Salmon River gorge is an unforgettable experience, with 100-foot drops from trail's edge to river's depths. This is a good Level I trail as long as the drop-offs don't bother you.

THE TRAIL: Your goal is an open camping area next to Fritzer Creek 5½ miles in. Start with a full canteen, as there is no good water source for the first 3 miles. The trail is big and beautiful but suffers from the vice of most streamside trails — a tendency to gain and lose altitude unnecessarily. The first possible campsites are on a large river bar just before the tramway. Here you have your choice of camping on pine-needle-covered ground or white sand. This would be a bad place to build a fire, as the needles are very dry and the sand is very white.

Just past here is the narrowest stretch of river and the site of an old bridge. Near here a 1949 vintage fire jumped the river. The stretch of trail from Slide Creek to Pidgeon Creek has a mostly northern exposure, and you walk through a dark, green, moist area. There are campsites when you round the bend past Pidgeon Creek, where the canyon opens up. This would be a good day-hiker's stopping place. As you cross Grave Creek you enter the Fritzer Ranch, and Fritzer Ford appears on the right. The trail passes just below the cabin and then crosses Fritzer Creek. It climbs beside the creek a short way and then cuts back to the right to reach an open area that has the last campsites on the left side of the river. The trail continues for 2 more miles.

EXTENSIONS: The Tailholt-Blue Lake Trail, which leaves near the tramway, leads all the way to the Secesh River, giving access along the way to the headwaters of Fritzer Creek. Hiking this steep trail would require a strong commitment of time and energy.

ACCESS: Drive 100 miles north from Scenic Junction on ID-55 to the Lick Creek Road in McCall (the yellow blinker downtown). Turn right here, left at the red blinker, and right at the yellow blinker by the golf course. After 2 miles bear right on the dirt road to Yellow Pine. After 31 miles the South Fork Road turns left, just before the second Secesh River bridge. The trailhead is 3½ miles down the road. There are Forest Service campgrounds on the Lick Creek Road and campsites 2 miles down the trail.

Another route that opens earlier in the season goes via Warm Lake. Drive 72 miles north from Scenic Junction to the Warm Lake Road and turn right. Turn left at the junction just across the bridge, on the South Fork Salmon River Road. Turn left on the Yellow Pine Road after 31½ miles, and drive one mile to the South Fork Road, where you turn right.

Salmon River Gorge — South Fork of Salmon River

LOON LAKE

HIKES: D, O, W, L.
TOTAL DISTANCE, O: 10 Miles.
DIFFICULTY: LEVEL I.
SEASON: June 10 — September 13.
USGS MAP: Loon Lake.
USFS MAP: McCall Ranger District
   (Payette N.F.).
MILEAGE: 137½ (8 Dirt).

INTRODUCTION: The trails to Loon Lake are very well maintained and open early in the season. While motorcyclists like these trails, the lake area has been included in the RARE II endorsed Lick Creek Wilderness Area. The trail, improved for motorbikes, makes easy Level I hiking. The murder of five Chinese miners near Loon Lake in 1879 touched off the Sheepeater War (though whites, not Indians, may have done the deed).

THE TRAIL: Loon Lake, 5 miles in via the East Side Secesh River Trail, can be reached by day-hikers and overnighters. A loop hike via the West Side Secesh River Trail can be completed as soon as the river can be forded. Just after starting, you cross a creek whose waters you should use if you camp in the campgrounds. Just past the next stream, Alex Creek, are some possible campsites. Although the Secesh drops 162 feet from the trailhead to the bridge, you will have to climb (and lose) at least twice that elevation on the way to the bridge. After crossing the river you climb to an exceptionally dense lodgepole pine forest. When the trail levels out it cuts right and climbs a moraine, avoiding a wet meadow — to protect it from you and you from it. After crossing a creek you come to some campsites and a trail divide. Loon Lake lies to the left, and the West Side

Trail lies to the right. There are campsites by the lake before and beyond the log crossing of Loon Creek.

The return loop trail on the river's west side is a sheer delight: a wide, smooth route that zips along through open lodgepole forests, crossing creeks and bogs on nifty log bridges. At last an unsigned trail, adorned by remnants of blue flagging, curves off to the right. This trail descends to the ford right at the campground. The trail emerges due south of the campground outhouse.

EXTENSIONS: You may leave the Loon Lake area via the Loon Creek, Victor Creek, or East or West Side Secesh River trails.

ACCESS: Drive 101 miles up ID-55 from Scenic Junction to the Warren Wagon Road north of McCall. Turn right and follow the road 35¼ miles (¾ miles past the second Secesh River bridge). Turn right at the sign for the Chinook Campground and drive 1¼ miles to the campground/trailhead. (This is a new road, different from that on your maps, that avoids a stream crossing and a wet meadow.)

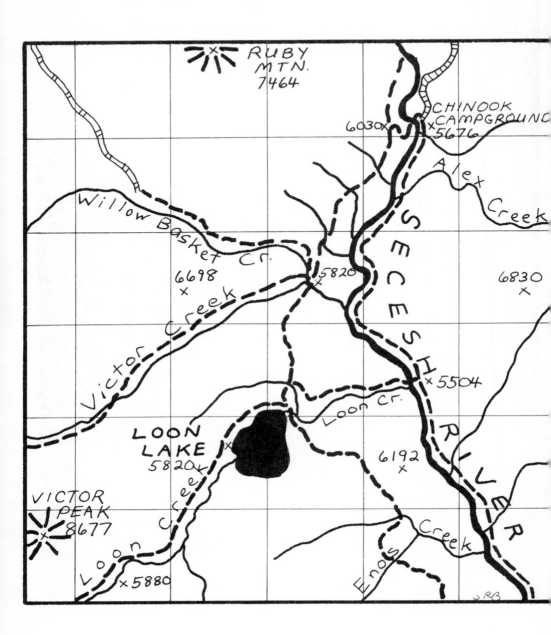

Looking up Loon Creek across Loon Lake

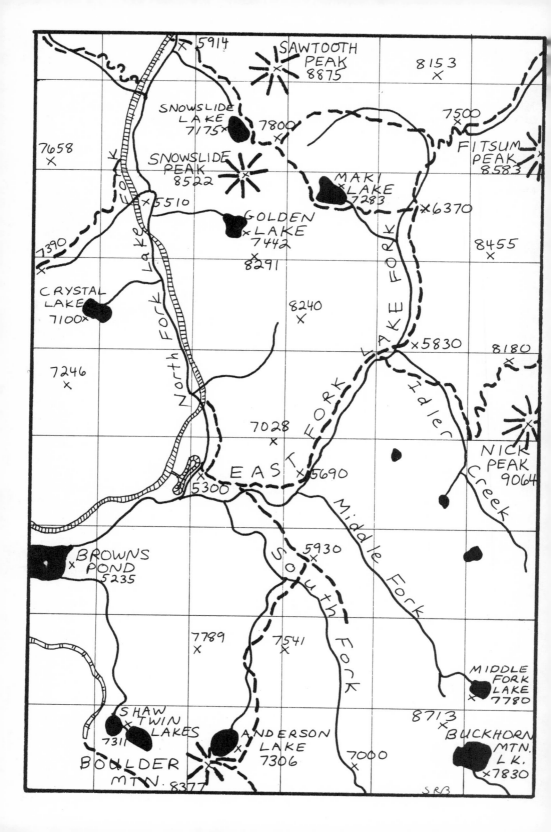

EAST FORK LAKE FORK

HIKES: D, O, W, L.
TOTAL DISTANCE, W: 15 Miles.
DIFFICULTY: Levels I, II, III.
SEASON: June 10 — October 1.
USGS MAP: Fitsum Summit.
USFS MAP: McCall Ranger District (Payette N.F.).
MILEAGE: 110 (7 Dirt).

INTRODUCTION: This readily accessible and well-trailed area nevertheless offers a chance to be alone. The East Fork Lake Fork has five tributary streams with trails running at least partway up them. These side creeks and the main stream all provide scenics and solitude. Travel up the Lake Fork Trail as far as the first crossing is Level I; beyond there it is Level III.

THE TRAIL: Level III hikers will want to make a loop to Maki Lake, over Snowslide Summit, and down the headwaters of the East Fork. Overnighters, day-hikers, and less experienced hikers can stop somewhere before the first crossing, 5½ miles in. The hike starts with a crossing of Lake Fork. (This crossing can be avoided by driving another mile up the Lick Creek Road to a bridge over Lake Fork and then hiking an extra mile along the east side of the creek.) After a short climb you come to the Boulder Lake Trail junction. Anderson Lake is 4 steep miles to the right, Boulder Lake 2 miles farther. Bear left here and continue up the East Fork. Beginning where the Middle Fork joins the East Fork, and continuing on to Idler Creek, there are many campsites along the trail. There are probably trails heading up these two creeks. USFS maps show no trail on the Middle Fork, while USGS maps do. A Forest Service sign simply says "Middle Fork." The Idler Creek Trail shows on both maps, but there is no trail sign.

After crossing the East Fork the trail becomes rough and rocky, and campsites become scarce. The Maki Lake turnoff comes 1½ miles later. The climb to this lake, which opens July 1, is a rugged one. The trail gains the 900 feet to the lake with great dispatch! After crossing the creek, go left and watch for a prominently blazed tree with a "Trail" sign. Go past the tree a short distance and you will see a small drainage coming down the rocks. This drainage is your trail. Go up to a bench, go left, and then cut back to the right and climb.

The trail is not hard to follow from here, though blazes are few, faint, and far between. As it climbs to the west it crosses a pretty little stream with a mini-waterfall and gives good views of North Fitsum Summit and Idler Creek. A view of Maki Lake's outlet creek signals a turn to the right for the trail, and it now follows a ridgeline. It doesn't cross the creek until you have a view of the level area around the lake. There are campsites below and above Maki Lake, which has been trammeled by man. The lake was raised by a dam, which washed out (catastrophically, it appears from the stream banks below).

The trail to Snowslide Summit is poorly marked, but you should have no trouble reaching the saddle between 8,151 feet and Snowslide Peak, as the route climbs on an open southern exposure. Once at the saddle, turn left and watch for a large dead tree with several generations of blazes still visible. Here the East Fork Lake Fork trail descends, and the Snowslide Trail goes north to Snowslide Lake and the Lick Creek Road. The trail down the East Fork to the Maki Lake turnoff has been ravaged by sheep grazing and becomes faint when it crosses meadows. There are few campsites along it.

EXTENSIONS: You could make a loop by going over North Fitsum Summit and returning by Fitsum Summit. Or you could lose yourself on one of Lake Fork's several tributaries.

ACCESS: Drive 100 miles from Scenic Junction on ID-55 to the Lick Creek Road in McCall. Turn right, then left at a red blinker, then right at a yellow blinker. Three miles from the highway turn right on the dirt road that leads to Yellow Pine.

After 6½ miles you come to the Lake Fork Campground, where you turn right. Now take left turns until you arrive at the trailhead sign. The first campsites on the trail are a long mile in.

East Fork of Lake Fork — headwaters view

RAINBOW RIDGE

HIKES: O, W, L.
TOTAL DISTANCE, W: 15 Miles.
DIFFICULTY: Level III.
SEASON: June 25 — September 25.
USGS MAPS: Parks Peak, Caton Lake.
USFS MAP: Krassel Ranger District
   (Payette N.F.).
MILEAGE: 148½ (45 Dirt).

INTRODUCTION: Hikers who venture into the mountains above the South Fork Salmon River and its East Fork will find extremely challenging conditions. River-to-ridge verticals over 4,000 feet are common, and trails deteriorate rapidly in the highly erosive soils. But the Rainbow Ridge Trail and the hike to Parks Peak are worth the effort. The Ridge Trail passes through a burned area that offers splendid vistas of distant mountains, the pattern of reforestation, and a rare natural arch. The view from 8,833-foot Parks Peak, once a lookout site, extends over an endless world of mountains and valleys. Level III skills are necessary to hike this rugged region, where often it is deer, not men, who keep the trails open. Travel in the burned area can be hazardous on windy days.

THE TRAIL: The best route ascends the Parks Peak Trail, goes west on the Rainbow Ridge Trail, and descends on the South Fork Sheep Creek Trail, returning to the Yellow Pine Road 2¼ miles from the starting point. Overnight hikers may make the level area near 6,940 feet their goal, while day-hikers should avoid this area in favor of the nearby South Fork Salmon River Trail. The 6,940-foot area also makes a good base for the hike to Parks Peak.

Take the ditched-out road up to a level,
logged area. Then head left to the small drainage shown on the USGS map. A steep, old skid path marks the start of your climb, which is shown accurately on the Caton Lake quadrangle. There are no campsites along the trail to 6,940 feet, a good place to camp on Friday night if you plan to hike the Rainbow Ridge loop.

The two USGS maps, produced six years apart, are confusing in this area. The Parks Peak map does not show the best trail to that summit, which cuts right from an easy-to-spot (though unsigned) trail junction below 6,940 and then crosses Parks Creek. It climbs to a meadow, crosses the creek, and joins the trail shown on the Parks Peak map. There are campsites near the ruins of an old cabin across Parks Creek from 6,940.

Use the trail that passes the old cabin to reach Parks Peak. There are more possible campsites by a possibly flowing stream below the saddle at 8,220. While the trail the USFS map shows heading west from this saddle doesn't seem to exist, the one heading east to Parks Peak is there and easy to follow. The last rocky steps to the old lookout site are marked by a faded orange stripe.

To hike the Rainbow Ridge loop, turn left at the trail divide below 6,940. After a short climb, a side trail descends left to a trashy hunter's camp. The trail divide you seek (shown on the Parks Peak map at 7,500 feet) is not signed, but prominent blazes mark the two routes. Turn left and climb to the Reegan Creek drainage, where a mixture of standing dead trees, solo live trees, wild flowers, and northern exposure timber makes a unique foreground for the view up Caton Creek.

Instead of neatly contouring along at 8,000 feet, the trail passes some possible ridgeline campsites and then drops down to Reegan Creek and water. It then climbs back to 8,000 feet and works its way under "Rock" to a signed trail divide. Bear left here and put on your thinking cap, for the descent from 8,015 is hard to follow. The trail once switchbacked down to the trees, but it is very faint now. Make

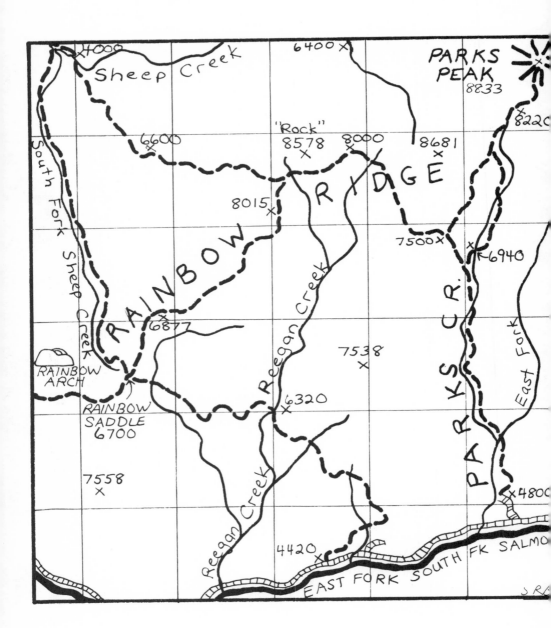

Sheep Creek

×4000

6400 ×

PARKS
PEAK
8833

8220

South Fork Sheep Creek

6600

"Rock"
8578
×

8000
×

8681
×

R A I N B O W   R I D G E

8015
×

7500 ×

×
×6940

×6877

RAINBOW
ARCH

RAINBOW
SADDLE
6700

Reegan Creek

7538
×

×6320

P A R K S   C R.

East Fork

7558
×

Reegan Creek

×4800

4420
×

EAST FORK SOUTH FK SALMO

J R

66

Old lookout site on Parks Peak — Rainbow Ridge

sure you are on the trail when you enter the woods!

After a long descent on the ridge, a switchback brings you to the saddle just below 6,877 feet. You may camp here by the trail or next to the creek not far to the south. The only other campsites with water are at the 6,400-foot level on the South Fork Sheep Creek north of Rainbow Saddle. You can get your long-awaited view of Rainbow Rock from the ridge between 6,877 and 6,918, where there are dry campsites. The arch is on the upper right edge of the largest, longest, lowest white rock across Sheep Creek.

Descent from Rainbow Saddle to the East Fork Salmon River is a difficult one. The trail traverses the upper Reegan Creek drainage, descending to and climbing from several streams before at last beginning the true descent via switchbacks. Despite the southern exposure, there are several water sources along the way. At last you come to an old road. Turn right, and after a short distance you will see a trail descending left to the Yellow Pine Road.

EXTENSIONS: You could continue west on the Rainbow Ridge Trail to Williams Peak Lookout and then descend to the road. Or you could descend one of the Sheep Creek trails to the South Fork Salmon River Trail. The most challenging hike would be to cross-country from Parks Peak to the magnificent Elk Creek drainage and link up with one of the trails there.

ACCESS: Follow directions for the South Fork Salmon River as far as the second Secesh River bridge. Continue straight toward Yellow Pine for 12 miles to reach the first trailhead, for the Sheep Creek Trail. A distinctive crooked ponderosa pine marks the unsigned trailhead. Use your USGS map to locate this and the next trailhead (Caton Creek makes a good landmark for this purpose). The Parks Peak trailhead, also unsigned, is 2¼ miles farther. The trail starts as a four-wheel-drive road. There are many pull-off campsites along the Yellow Pine Road, and a few Forest Service campgrounds.

COUNCIL MOUNTAIN

HIKES: D, O.
TOTAL DISTANCE, O: 7 Miles.
DIFFICULTY: Level III.
SEASON: June 25 — October 1.
USGS MAP: Council (1:62,500).
USFS MAP: Council Ranger District (Payette N.F.).
MILEAGE: 110½ (16 Dirt).

INTRODUCTION: Council Mountain is eight miles east of the town of Council and a mile higher. The peak is surrounded by tributaries of the Weiser River. Twenty-five years ago a wilderness stretched for 20 miles southeast from the mountain, including all of West Mountain and much of the Middle Fork Weiser River. Now a road follows that river to its source, and logging roads have obliterated the trailheads of the Granite Creek and Cabin Creek trails along the river. Heavy cattle grazing has made the trails in the area difficult to follow, so they are Level III.

THE TRAIL: The best hike is a 7-mile loop that takes you to Granite Basin, the old Council Lookout site, and the head of the North Fork Cottonwood Creek. If you can carry enough water to camp overnight, you may do so along the way.

Hike on the road about ½ mile from the washout to the trail sign, where the river pinches off the road. Take the rightmost trail that climbs the bank. After crossing two side creeks the trail crosses the river itself. From the meadows that follow this crossing you can see the buttelike formation of Columbia River basalt, whose snowfields feed the river far into summer.

There is actually a switchback to help you up to the East Fork-Granite Creek di-vide. The view is good from here, with Granite Basin (and possible campsites) at your feet, but if you climb to the right it will better. There is a trail divide at the end of this climb, on the ridgetop. To the left of here is the old lookout site, easily identifiable from the mess left behind. The view from here embraces the Seven Devils and Lick Creek mountains, and the North Fork Payette, Little Salmon, and Weiser River valleys.

Back at the ridgetop junction, go down to the west. Cattle have thoroughly ob-scured the route down to the Mill Creek Trail. Time and again you will ask your-self the question that has troubled the most brilliant bovine philosophers — right or left? Your only guides are primitive posts the Forest Service put up years ago, many of which have now fallen. You can safely assume that the cattle have devised a superior system to simplify *their* route-finding decisions. If only they could pass it on to the USFS!

A right turn on the Mill Creek Trail will take you to a still-standing post that is above and north of Log Cabin Creek. From here head for a low pole and a gap at the end of a bare ridge, before it becomes fringed with trees. After the gap the trail traverses across the heads of two drainages before it returns to the East Fork. The first is Larkspur Gulch, the second the North Fork Cottonwood Creek. Each of these creeks is supposed to have a trail running along the ridge to its east. The trail east of Larkspur Gulch (which the USGS map calls the Mill Creek Trail) is in good con-dition. The trail east of the North Fork Cottonwood Creek (which the USFS map calls the Mill Creek Trail) is in poor con-dition. There are campsites in the North Fork drainage.

Your loop concludes with a descent from the notch overlooking the East Fork Weiser River. A trail shows on the USGS map and not on the USFS map, but it ex-ists and is easy to follow. It is not the one that contours to the right (looking for greener pastures). You want the trail that descends just left of the drainage that leaves the notch. For a while it goes down at a moderate pace, but then it takes a nose dive to reach a meadow. From there you can continue straight down to the East Fork Trail, or you may descend to the left to intersect an old road, which leads back to your car. The clear-cut you parked by makes a good landmark.

EXTENSIONS: You might continue south from the old lookout site along the Cabin Creek Trail, which peters out in a logged area above Cabin Creek Campground.

ACCESS: The easiest access is by the East Fork Weiser River Road. Drive 41 miles from the Meridian exit on I-84 to Exit 3, and turn right on US-95. Go north to Council, and 10 miles from the center of town turn right on the East Fork Road.

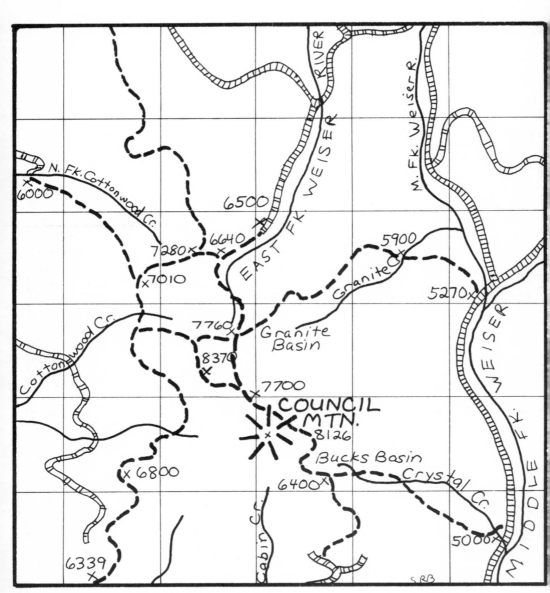

Follow the road all the way up the river, crossing it and then turning left just past the bridge. This is the road in the northeast corner of your USGS map. It has been shallowly ditched out for the first mile and then washed out near a clear-cut. Park here. There are campsites along the road before and after the washout.

You can also reach the trailhead from Donnelly, 86 miles north of Scenic Junction on ID-55. Follow signs for Council, crossing No Business Saddle and turning right on the Middle Fork Weiser River Road. After 5 twisting miles on this road turn left on a side road that can be muddy, which leads you to the East Fork Weiser River Road, where you turn left.

Butte view — Council Mountain

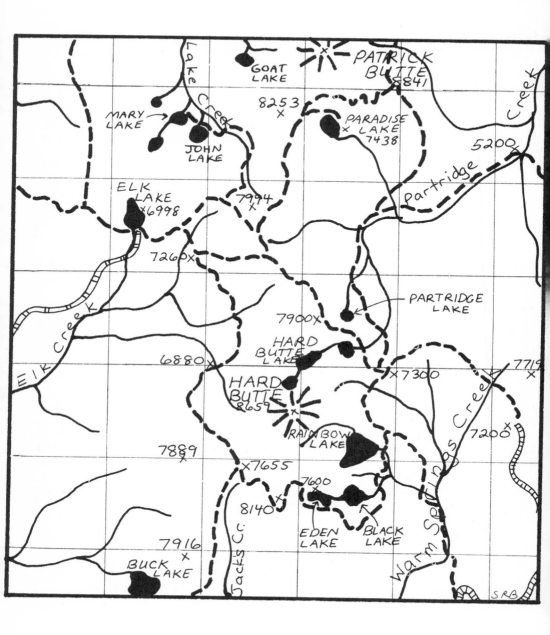

GOAT LAKE

PATRICK BUTTE
8841

8253
X

PARADISE
LAKE
X 7438

5200
X

Lake Creek

MARY LAKE

JOHN LAKE

Partridge Creek

ELK LAKE
X6998

7994
X

7260X

PARTRIDGE LAKE

7900X

HARD BUTTE LAKE

6880 X

X 7300

7719
X

Elk Creek

HARD BUTTE
8659
X

RAINBOW LAKE

7889
X

X7655

7600
X

7200
X

8140

EDEN LAKE

BLACK LAKE

Warm Springs Creek

7916
X

BUCK LAKE

Jacks Cr.

SRB

AROUND HARD BUTTE

HIKES: D, O, W, L.
TOTAL DISTANCE, W: 15 Miles.
DIFFICULTY: Levels I, II, III.
SEASON: July 4 — October 1.
USGS MAPS: Patrick Butte, Hazard Lake.
USFS MAP: New Meadows Ranger District
(Payette N.F.).
MILEAGE: 158 (27 Dirt).

INTRODUCTION: The Hazard Lake Road, a high-quality dirt road, leads to many fine hiking areas north of McCall. To the west of the road are Grass Mountain, Granite Peak, and Hard and Patrick buttes. To the east are Lava Butte and Little French Creek. A good trail net serves all these areas, with hikes varying in difficulty from the easy walks to Twin or Grass Mountain lakes to the switchback extravaganzas of the Patrick Butte area. RARE II unaccountably passed over this outstanding area. Access to the Hard Butte Lakes on the mountain's east side is Level I hiking; completing the loop presents route-finding problems requiring Level III skills. Cattle graze the west side of Hard Butte every other year. Check with the Forest Service if you don't desire their company.

THE TRAIL: Skilled weekenders may hike the 15-mile loop around Hard Butte. Day-hikers and overnighters can hike to the Hard Butte Lakes, 4 miles in, or to Rainbow Lake, 3 miles in. The trail you start on looks more like a road (and despite "Road Closed" signs, jeeps sneak around Forest Service barriers to enter the area). After a short mile a recognizable trail veers to the left of the road. Take it, for it rejoins the road a mile or so later. A half mile farther you come to Warm Springs Saddle and a trail junction. Here you have a choice: the loop route and Rainbow Lake are to the left, the Hard Butte Lakes straight ahead.

Here, too, you begin to see spray-painted orange blazes. The author likes these markings for poorly maintained, little-used trails that follow rocky routes with few trees to blaze. The USFS doesn't like them since they are "unnatural" (and since, in this case, the trail crew didn't always get things just right.) At any rate, they come in handy time and again on the loop route.

The trail is easier to follow from the saddle to the Hard Butte Lakes (called Twin Lakes on the Forest Service map). There is one short, rocky climb to a trail divide, where you again go straight. The next big creek drains the lakes. Go left and follow it, staying on the south side of the lakes to reach the best campsites.

The left fork from Warm Springs Saddle leads to Rainbow Lake and the loop route — which is easier to follow when made in a clockwise manner. The trail passes a cow camp and then comes to the signed Rainbow Lake turnoff. There are many campsites on this stretch of trail.

After crossing Rainbow Lake Creek the trail stays level until it comes to the next drainage, where it gives you a choice of routes. You may descend to the left, drop into the drainage, cross the creek, and climb through trees to the border of a meadow. An alternative route descends to the right, crosses the creek near the end of the trees, and climbs to the edge of the meadow and the trail. There is camping in the trees on both routes.

Climb in the open until you come to Black Lake Creek. The lake is not far off the trail and offers some campsites. The trail then climbs to a neat level area where it cuts right and follows a devious route through a stretch of pure granite. At last you come to Eden Lake, a small marshy affair in a large meadow with a few campsites. Follow the left side of the meadow to its far end and then climb straight to the last meadow. The trail goes to the right from here and scrambles to the ridgeline.

At the top you are greeted by a fine view of the Seven Devils, the Hazard Creek gorge, and the area you will hike through. Go left along the ridge, cut right at a sign to descend to a large meadow, and then contour to the saddle at the head of Jack's Creek.

From here to the junction with the Elk Lake Trail the route is rough and hard to follow. As you descend you pass between granite and basalt, cross a stream, and then find yourself descending traillessly down an open ridge. Bear right when you cross the first of two meadows, where you may camp. You should pick up the trail again at the edge of the second meadow. After crossing a stream you enter a Black Forest, a dense stand of spruce. Once through the woods, the work begins as you climb a rocky stretch and come out in a meadow. On the north end of it are some eroding trail-bike scars. Hike toward them and you will see your trail to the left as it climbs to meet the Elk Lake Trail. Turn right at the junction and climb on the trail. It will take you to the Hard Butte Lakes and your car.

EXTENSIONS: You could extend this loop to the north by trying one of the rugged trails around Patrick Butte.

ACCESS: From Scenic Junction, drive 105½ miles to the Hazard Lake/Brundage Mountain Road and turn right. Follow signs to Hazard Lake, bearing left when the pavement ends at the ski area road and again at the Brundage Reservoir Road. Pass up Hazard Lake, bear left at the Elk Meadows Road, and stop at the road's end — your trailhead. There is camping at Hazard Lake, along the road, and along the trail just past the trailhead.

Hard Butte — poor old Eden Lake

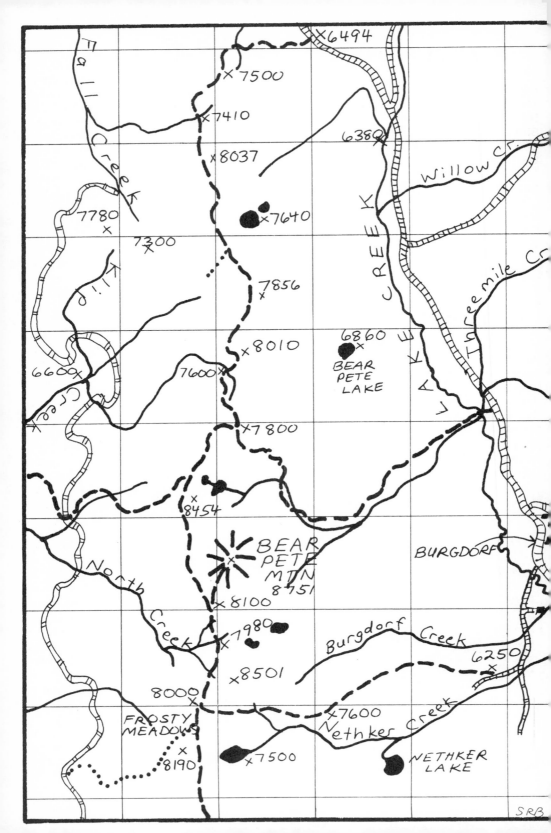

BEAR PETE RIDGE

HIKES: D, O, W, L.
TOTAL DISTANCE, W: 14 Miles.
DIFFICULTY: Levels II, III.
SEASON: July 1 — September 13.
USGS MAP: Burgdorf (1:62,500).
USFS MAP: McCall Ranger District (Payette N.F.).
MILEAGE: 138½ (9¼ Dirt).

INTRODUCTION: Bear Pete Mountain dominates the view from the historic mining town of Burgdorf. The ridge extending north and south of Bear Pete is a survivor, an island of backcountry in a sea of roads and clear-cuts. Hopefully the "limited forest development" the Forest Service has planned for this ridge will retain its excellent wilderness qualities. The Bear Pete Trail is 14 miles long and may be viewed as two separate hikes or one long one that ends 8 miles from its beginning. The northern segment that starts at Toller Ditch is Level II; the southern segment that uses the Nethker Trail is Level III.

THE TRAILS: From Toller Ditch day-hikers and overnighters can hike 2 miles to a level area of trees and meadows. Weekenders may go as far south as the Pete Creek Trail junction, 7 miles in, before turning back. The starting climb, while steep, is made on a good dirt trail that often divides and reunites. Rest assured as long as the trail you follow goes *up*. After crossing a creek you enter a level timbered area ideal for remote camping. A large meadow lies to the left of the trail here, the overnighter's goal.

A descent to a stream marks the end of this easy going. From the creek you must climb straight ahead (not on the nice neat switchbacks the USGS map shows). Your reward for this effort is a spectacular view that stretches west to the Seven Devils. If you carry a compass and a New Meadows Ranger District map you can identify many features. As you continue to hike along the ridge you will spot many possible dry camps. One bad spot comes as you pass above the Klip Creek-Fall Creek divide. A trail descends to the right, while your route climbs a bit to the left and stays high. As you approach the Pete Creek saddle, the trail does a funny thing. Instead of using the saddle, it makes an abrupt descent to a flowing creek and then climbs back to the saddle, where you may camp. To continue south, go east on the Pete Creek Trail until it starts to descend. A poor trail then cuts back to the right and climbs towards Bear Pete Mountain.

The southern approach uses the Nethker Creek Trail, which climbs to the Frosty Meadows area. Day-hikers may hike 3 miles to the first water and a magnificent view, while overnighters must climb another mile to reach a campsite. Weekenders may proceed 7 miles north to the Pete Creek saddle (or the full 15 miles to Toller Ditch).

For the first 1,300 feet you hike a good trail along a dry ridgeline, with dry camps off in the trees. Then you make a short descent and enter a changed environment. Your nice, shady trail becomes a rocky, exposed route that traverses a mountainside and looks down on upper Nethker Creek. After crossing a creek (the day-hiker's goal), the climb gets even steeper. Once on top you enter a region of intensely green meadows that dot the west flank of Bear Pete Ridge. There are many campsites in this area, from which you can make the climb to Bear Pete Mountain or the hike to Pete Creek saddle. As you hike along the mountain's west border you have the same fine Seven Devils view you get to the north. You can also look back to emerald green Frosty Meadows.

EXTENSIONS: You may choose two different exits to the south: Josephine Lake or Squaw Meadows. All trails that descend west towards French Creek will be obscured by logging along a new road.

ACCESS: Drive 101 miles north on ID-55 from Scenic Junction to the Warren Wagon Road, where you turn right. Drive 28½ miles to the Burgdorf turnoff at the pavement's end. Turn left here, and for the Toller Ditch trailhead drive 9¼ miles toward Riggins. For the Nethker Trail turn left on the Burgdorf Guard Station Road after 1½ miles and right on the Nethker Trail Road after ¾ miles. The trailhead is ¼ mile beyond. There is a Forest Service campground in Burgdorf, and there are other roadside campsites in the area.

Bear Pete Mountain — Bear Pete and Burgdorf

THE NEEDLES TRAIL

HIKES: D, O, W, L.
TOTAL DISTANCE, W: 14 Miles.
DIFFICULTY: Level II.
SEASON: June 30 — October 1.
USGS MAPS: Gold Fork (1:62,500), Blackmare.
USFS MAP: McCall Ranger District (Payette N.F.).
MILEAGE: 109½ (15½ Dirt).

INTRODUCTION: East of McCall the Lick Creek Range forms the divide between the North Fork Payette and the South Fork Salmon rivers. While the highest peak in the range, Nick, barely tops 9,000 feet, local relief is often in the 3,000-foot range, and trails commonly start by proceeding up broad valleys and end by climbing over steep passes. The southern boundary of these mountains is marked by the Needles, a group of spires that dominates the Gold Fork River drainage. An easy entry into the Lick Creek Range is by way of the Needles Trail, one of three that leave the Kennally Creek Campground. It is easy to follow as it gradually climbs 2,300 feet to Needles Summit; Level II.

THE TRAIL: Your goal is a unique flat area below Square Top Mountain at the head of Gold Fork River. Overnight hikers can stop at one of the dry campsites along the way, while day-hikers may do better on the flatter East Fork or North Fork Kennally Creek trails.

A mile from the campground the trail divides. Go right on the East Fork Kennally Creek Trail for another mile to the Needles Trail junction. Go right and cross Kennally Creek, which you may have to ford in early season. There are campsites over the creek and through the lodgepoles.

After an initial rocky stretch the trail levels off, traversing the west side of a ridge but gaining altitude all the time. On the east side of this ridge lies Blackmare Lake, and a sign marks the path to the lake. This route, not hard to follow, involves a steep 500-foot climb, a scenic stretch that crosses a rock field, and an easy pass over a saddle and down to two upper lakes, where there is camping. The route then makes a 500-foot "high dive" to the Blackmare Creek Trail, which then climbs 300 feet to the lake, where there is little camping.

The first water along the Needles Trail comes right after the Blackmare cutoff. There is a campsite just past here, and campsites continue to follow streams until you come to Stump Lake Creek. This creek leads you to Needles Summit, passing Stump Lake, which has many campsites and no fish. The lake area would make a good base for the rugged hike south to the Needles.

The trail deteriorates past Needles Summit, becoming rocky, Level III, but superscenic. You look down on an unnamed, untamed tributary of the Gold Fork; across to Gold Fork Rock and the Needles; and, if you climb to the ridgeline to the left, down on Blackmare Lake and north to Blackmare Peak. The trail ends its lazy contour on this southern exposure with a short but unsweet stretch of switchbacks. They take you to a unique tableland below Square Top Mountain at the very source of Gold Fork River. While campsites are numerous here, water can be a problem, for the two streams that drain the area may not flow in late season. In that case, descend the southern of the two until it does flow.

EXTENSIONS: Loop hikes from here continue to the South Fork Blackmare cutoff and return to the campground via either Blackmare Summit and East Fork Kennally Creek or Cougar Saddle and North Fork Kennally Creek. Or you could continue south on the Needles Trail to Gold Fork Rock.

ACCESS: Start at Scenic Junction. Take ID-55 94 miles north and turn right on the Paddy Flat Road. Follow signs to Kennally Creek Campground, the trailhead. There are campsites along the first two miles of trail.

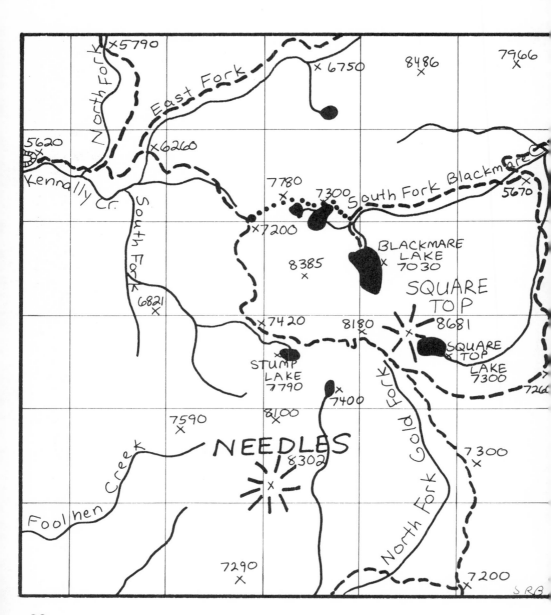

Needles Trail — Blackmare Lake and Square Top Mountain

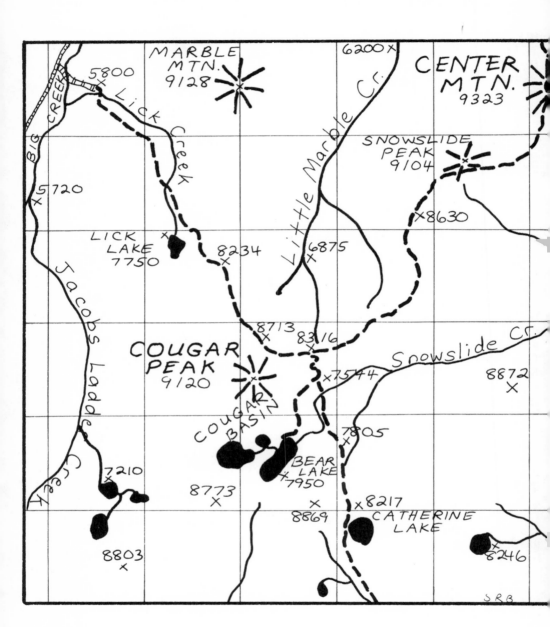

MARBLE
MTN.
9128

6200 X

CENTER
MTN.
9323

5800
X

Lick Creek

Little Marble Cr.

SNOWSLIDE
PEAK
9104
X

BIG CREEK

X 5720

X 8630

LICK
LAKE
7750
X

8234
X

X 6875

Jacobs Ladder Creek

8713
X

83 16
X

Snowslide Cr.

COUGAR
PEAK
9120
X

X 7544

8872
X

COUGAR BASIN

7210
X

7805
X

BEAR
LAKE
7950
X

8773
X

X
8869

X 8217

CATHERINE
LAKE

8803
X

X
8246

SRB

82

COUGAR BASIN

HIKES: O, W, L.
TOTAL DISTANCE, W: 15 Miles.
DIFFICULTY: Level III.
SEASON: July 10 — September 13.
USGS MAP: Edwardsburg.
USFS MAP: Big Creek Ranger District
  (Payette N.F.).
MILEAGE: 172½ (69 Dirt).

INTRODUCTION: The River of No Return Wilderness Area (RNRWA) has kept its primitive character because of its remoteness and its immensity. The few trailheads lie mostly at the end of long drives over dirt roads, and the number of good weekend hikes is limited. Cougar Basin, near the remote Big Creek Ranger Station, is a popular destination for summer hikers and fall hunters. The latter usually leave a mess that doesn't contribute to "that wild feeling," a mess that backpackers should remove for their less-enlightened fellow wilderness users. The hike to Cougar is a pretty one, though, that imparts a sense of the size and variety of the RNRWA and serves as a jump-off point or base camp for longer trips. It is also a rugged weekend hike, with 3,300 feet of ascent and 1,200 feet of descent. Despite the generally good trail, this is a Level III hike.

THE TRAIL: Bear Lake in Cougar Basin is 7½ miles in. Overnight or lazy weekend hikers may stop at Lick Lake, 3 miles in. The trail offers little to day-hikers unless they are willing to reach Lick Lake. Fill your canteen as you cross Lick Creek, for the next 1,400 feet of climbing are on a dry trail. A mile past the next creek crossing you come to the un-signed Lick Lake turnoff. There are a few campsites by the lake.

After climbing to the saddle at 8,234 feet you have an excellent view of the glacial carved U-shaped valley of Little Marble Creek and of the three summits across the valley. Center Mountain is the timbered ridge to the left, Snowslide Peak the distinctive summit in the center. You may camp here or a little farther along the trail near a creek. A traverse and then a rocky climb bring you to 8,713 feet, from which point 17 switchbacks take you down to the meadow and trail divide at 7,544. Turn right on the Cougar Basin Trail and watch for the abrupt right turn and climb shown on the USGS map. There are many campsites at Bear Lake.

EXTENSIONS: A Cougar Basin camp could be used as a base for exploring the surrounding area. A day each could be spent in fishing the West Fork Monumental Creek lakes, moseying around the Pinnacles, and hiking the "trail" to Center Mountain. The Monumental Creek and Center Mountain trails can also be used for extended hikes into the heart of the RNRWA.

ACCESS: Drive to Yellow Pine by one of two routes: from Scenic Junction up ID-55 to the Lick Creek Road in McCall and then on to Yellow Pine; or up ID-55 to Cascade, then right to Warm Lake and Landmark, and then left to Yellow Pine. Go five miles east from Yellow Pine junction, following signs for Big Creek Ranger Station, and turn left on the Profile Summit-Big Creek Road. This road, while not too rough, is narrow and steep and demands caution. After 16½ miles you come to the Lick Lake Road, where you turn right and come to a ford of Big Creek. The trailhead is only ½ mile from here, so you don't have to ford in your car. Once across, go straight between the two fence lines to the trail sign. There are many campsites along the Big Creek Road and no camping along the trail until Lick Lake.

Cougar Basin — Bear Lake

Area Three

THE SEVEN DEVILS

An Indian legend tells of a young brave who encountered, one after another, seven devils while hunting in the mountains. Since then these mountains have been known as the Seven Devils, and several peaks have been named with the legend in mind. The Seven Devils Mountains should become better known, since they are now part of the Hells Canyon Wilderness Area. However, because the Forest Service named the wilderness Hells Canyon (the area used to be called the Hells Canyon-Seven Devils Scenic Area) images of 110-degree heat and abundant rattlesnakes may keep hikers away. Anyone who has hiked the Seven Devils high country knows it as a place of rugged trails, beautiful scenery, and changeable weather — but no rattlesnakes.

An excellent 28-mile loop runs around the range and can be reached from all three access points to the area — Rapid River, Windy Saddle, and Black Lake. This hike can be made in three days or three weeks, depending on how much time is spent hiking up creeks toward lakes or down creeks toward canyons. There is no water on the loop trail from Dog Creek to Baldy Lake Creek, an eight-mile stretch. Hells Canyon itself has an incomplete trail system with poor access from the south. Southern Idaho hikers who want to hike in the early season are much better off using the Rapid River Trail.

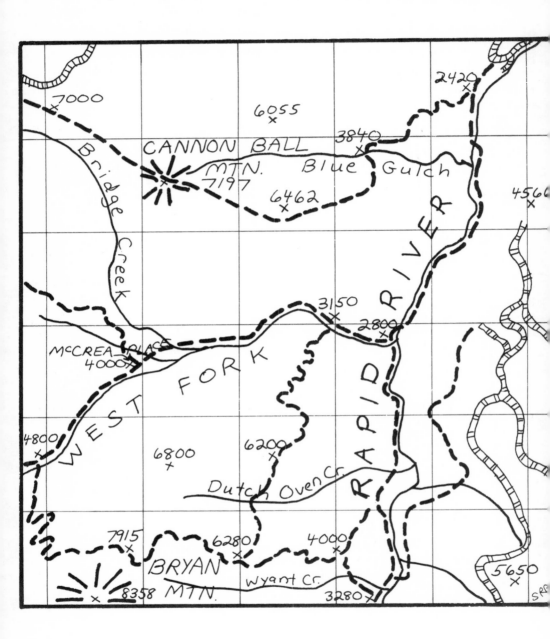

86

WEST FORK RAPID RIVER

HIKES: D, O, W, L.
TOTAL DISTANCE, W: 15 Miles.
DIFFICULTY: Levels I, II.
SEASON: March 15 — October 1.
USGS MAP: Heaven's Gate.
USFS MAP: Hells Canyon-Seven Devils
  Scenic Area (Payette, Nez Perce N.F.).
MILEAGE: 146 (3 Dirt).

INTRODUCTION: Rapid River is a federally designated wild river. The trail that runs along it, open all year long in its lower stretches, is especially beautiful in the spring, when biscuit-root colors the hills with yellow. While the main Rapid River is in a hurry to reach the Little Salmon, its West Fork makes positive haste to reach the main river. Despite giving it 26 out of 28 possible points on a wilderness quality scale, RARE II did not recommend this drainage for wilderness status. The trail is in excellent condition, with new bridges that were built in the wake of a recent flash flood. It is Level I as far as the West Fork, and Level II after that, when it climbs beside that stream.

THE TRAIL: Your goal is the area of the McRae Place, 7½ miles in. Day-hikers may stop at the West Fork, 4½ miles in, while overnighters will have to travel an extra half mile to reach a campsite. There are two roads at the trailhead; take the upper one that is marked with a sign. Advance confidently on the road, and take a trail whenever you have a choice between a trail and a road. You quickly enter the Rapid River gorge, which has few campsites but great scenery. Just past the second bridge, 4½ miles in, the trail and the river both divide. Turn right for the West Fork Trail. Prepare to climb — and climb!

A short distance beyond the point where the river stops falling and the trail stops climbing, the Potter Creek Trail cuts left and easily fords the West Fork. There is excellent camping here for overnighters.

There are a few more campsites on the way to the McRae Place, 2½ miles farther. There are a few tentsites around the cabin and many fine dry campsites around the Frank Wurl cabin. This old abode is reached by the trail that starts on the west side of the McRae Place, climbs on the left of the creek, crosses it, and then climbs to a grassy knoll and the cabin. The McRae Place marks the boundary between canyons and mountains, and there are rattlesnakes on the trail below it.

EXTENSIONS: A good loop hike would climb the Frank Wurl Trail to the Boise Trail in the Seven Devils, take it south to Horse Heaven, and then return by the West Fork Rapid River. Other loops can be made by hiking the West Fork to Bryan Mountain and then to the main Rapid River.

ACCESS: Take ID-55 from Scenic Junction to its junction with US-95 in New Meadows. Go 32 miles north on US-95 to the Rapid River Road, just across the bridge and marked by a sign for Idaho Power's Circle C fish hatchery. Drive 3 miles to the end of the road and park where two dirt roads head upcanyon. The upper road is the trailhead. No camping is allowed in the hatchery area, though you may be able to eke out a tentsite in the hills a short distance down the road (trail). An alternate route to New Meadows takes I-84 to US-95 near Payette and follows it north through Council.

West Fork of Rapid River — biscuit-root in bloom

UPPER RAPID RIVER LOOP

HIKES: D, O, W, L.
TOTAL DISTANCE, W: 20 Miles.
DIFFICULTY: Levels II, III.
SEASON: July 4 — October 1.
USGS MAPS: Cuprum*(1:62,500), Railroad Saddle*, Pollock Mountain.
USFS MAP: New Meadows Ranger District (Payette N.F.).
MILEAGE: 151 (16¼ Dirt).

INTRODUCTION: The upper Rapid River trail system has much to offer hikers. Trails along the river itself are closed to motor vehicles and feature excellent campsites. Trails on the open ridges above the river give panoramic views that present the Hard Butte, Lick Creek, Seven Devils, and Wallowa mountains in all their glory. Considering, too, the trails that lead to alpine lakes and to the lower Rapid River, this area is a complete ecosystem that should be added to the Hells Canyon Wilderness Area. Two different loop routes may be hiked from the Ant Basin trailhead. The shorter loop is a Level II hike, while the longer one is Level III because of route-finding problems.

THE TRAIL: The shorter loop, 14 miles long, descends to Rapid River via the North Star Trail and ascends via the Indian Springs Trail. The longer loop, 20 miles long, descends the North Star Trail, follows the Rapid River all the way to its source below Lick Creek Lookout, and returns via the lookout and the ridge. Dayhikers and overnighters can capture the outstanding scenery by hiking to Indian Springs or North Star Butte, 2½ miles in. Both loops begin with a 500-foot climb up a good trail to the Rapid River Ridge Trail. Start this climb with a full canteen. Turn right on the Ridge Trail and walk 2

miles, passing many dry ridgeline campsites. At the North Star Trail divide turn left and prepare for a stupendous view. Another good viewpoint on the way down is by the crag at 6,365 feet. Instead of taking a swan dive from here as the USGS map shows, the trail gets rough for a while and then begins a series of switchbacks that gently bring you to Rapid River. There are campsites at the confluence with Black Lake Creek, a short distance to the right.

Both loop routes go left from here, climbing near the river. There are no campsites on the 4 miles to the Indian Springs Trail junction, but there are many sites before and after the river crossing just past here. Short-loop hikers can ascend the Indian Springs Trail, turn right on the Rapid River Ridge Trail, and return to Ant Basin. Long-loop hikers will continue up Rapid River on a trail that has a nasty habit of disappearing every time it leaves the forest and enters a meadow. If you keep climbing across the meadows at the same rate you were climbing through the forest you will probably find the trail again in the trees on the far side. (Author's note: May The Force be with you !) Fill your canteen from one of the small creeks you cross before you climb to the dry ridge.

At last you reach that ridge at the Rapid River-Lick Creek saddle, where you could camp. Turn left and climb to the Lick Creek Lookout for views of the Wallowa Mountains — and everyplace else. The Rapid River Ridge Trail from here to the Ant Basin Trail is in poor condition. Three rules will help you stay on it: it rarely gains altitude, it prefers open country, and it stays on the east side of the ridge.

EXTENSIONS: A longer loop would take the Lake Fork Ridge Trail (not shown on any of the maps), which starts just across Rapid River from the North Star Trail, to Twin Lakes, Bear Saddle, and the Lick Creek Lookout. The whole Seven Devils trail system is accessible from Black Lake, at the head of Black Lake Creek.

ACCESS: Drive to Council via I-84 and US-95. Drive 20 miles north of downtown Council to the Price Valley Road, where you turn left. Follow signs for Boulder Creek, which is 11½ miles in. Just across the Boulder Creek bridge the Ant Basin Road leads to the left. After 4¾ miles the road narrows and crosses Ant Basin Creek. Park here and walk around the corner to the trailhead. The first campsites on the trail are on the ridge, one mile in; car campers will find good sites back along the Boulder Creek Road.

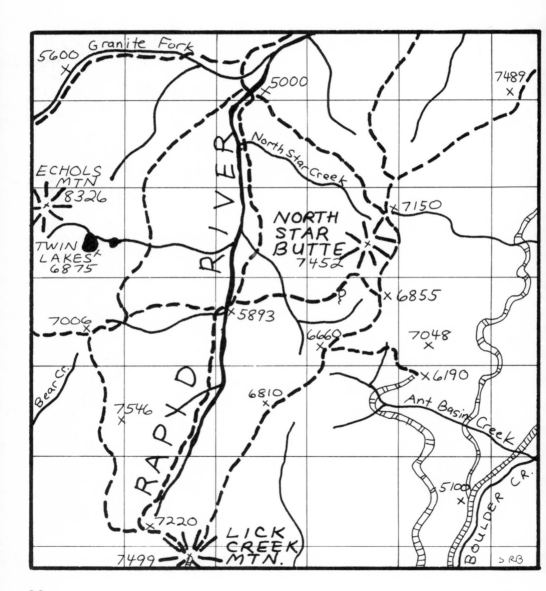

Looking downcanyon — Upper Rapid River loop

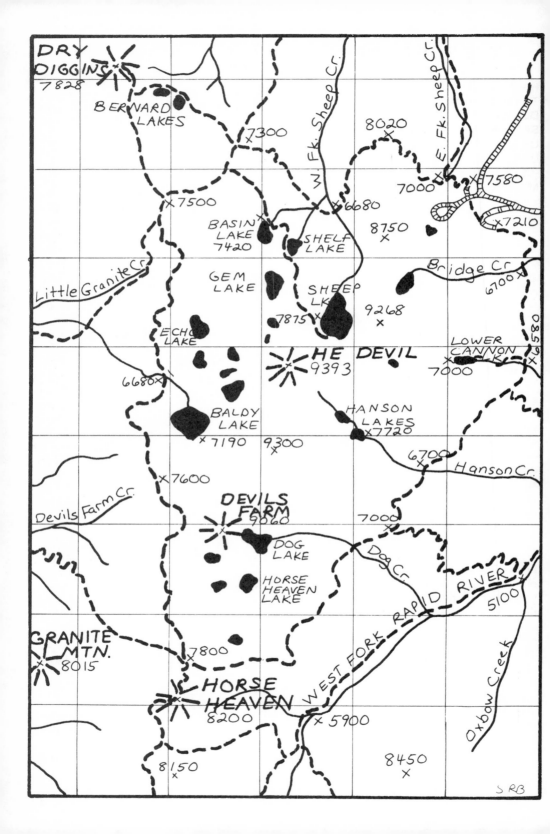

THE BOISE TRAIL

HIKES: D, O, W, L.
TOTAL DISTANCE, W: 16 Miles.
DIFFICULTY: Levels I, II, III.
SEASON: July 1 — October 1.
USGS MAP: He Devil (1:62,500).
USFS MAP: Hells Canyon-Seven Devils Scenic Area (Payette N.F.).
Mileage: 161 (17 Dirt).

INTRODUCTION: The east side of the Seven Devils offers excellent views of the Rapid River canyon below and of the Hard Butte-Patrick Butte area across the Little Salmon River. The Boise Trail, which follows an old packers' route, is a well constructed and maintained Level II trail. As it moves south it cuts across Cannon, Hanson, and Dog Creeks. There are campsites along each creek by the Boise Trail and also by the lakes which the three creeks drain. Lower Cannon Lake is reached by an easy Level I trail, but access to the Hanson, Dog, and Horse Heaven lakes is by Level III cross-country hiking.

THE TRAIL: Your goal is Dog Lake, 10 miles in. Overnight campers and day-hikers may go to Lower Cannon Lake, 4 miles in. From Windy Saddle parking lot you may take the trail or the roads down to the real trailhead at Seven Devils Guard Station. Follow the trail down to Bridge Creek, where there are a few campsites. The stretch of trail your USGS map shows climbing from Bridge Creek and descending to Cannon Creek has been replaced by one that contours the whole way. The Cannon Creek Trail is well marked, and there are many campsites at the lower lake. Most of the Cannon Creek valley burned in 1962, and travel on the trail is

hazardous during high winds due to the many snags.

The Boise Trail has no reliable campsites or water sources until it crosses Hanson Creek. The climb from the trail to the Hanson Lakes is a very tough one. Stay on the right margin of the trees until you leave the woods and come to rock. There are now two routes: up the creek, which is nasty and wet; or up a grassy stretch to the right, which is rough but passable. If you go to the right you will find stretches of steep switchback "trail." Just before you reach the lakes you come to a large level area with lots of room for campsites. From here, a short climb and a quick descent bring you to a tiny pond. To the left is the lower lake, which boasts a stunningly scenic outlet. The upper lake is straight ahead.

There are many more campsites on Dog Creek than on Hanson, and the trail to Dog Lake is easier to follow. After another improved stretch of trail from Hanson to Dog Creek, cross Dog and turn right. You quickly recross the creek and climb, passing more campsites. When you come to the tributary that flows from the lakeless northern cirque, hike on its right side for 50 yards before crossing. Once you reach Dog Creek, climb on its right side until it levels off. There are campsites on the left side of the lake all the way to the pond your USGS map shows.

EXTENSIONS: Horse Heaven Lake is 12 miles from Windy Saddle. From Horse Heaven you have three possible routes: north along the west side of the Seven Devils to Windy Saddle (a 28-mile loop), south to Black Lake, or northeast along the West Fork Rapid River.

ACCESS: Take ID-55 from Scenic Junction to its junction with US-95 at New Meadow. Turn right on US-95 and follow it for 33 miles to the Seven Devils Road. Turn left on this steep road and then bear left after 1½ miles. The crucial turnoff comes about 9½ miles from the highway, when the Seven Devils Road turns right and climbs. (The road you have been on goes straight and ends in a logging area.) After 6½ more miles a road signed "Administrative Area" leads left to the Seven Devils Guard Station and the actual trailhead. You may wish to drop off gear and people there, but you must park your car at Windy Saddle, a short distance past the guard station turnoff. The Seven Devils Campground is down the road to the left of Windy Saddle, but it is often full, and you may have to camp in the trailhead area. The first campsites along the trail are at Bridge Creek, one mile in.

Boise Trail — east side of Seven Devils (from Rapid River Ridge)

SHEEP CREEK LAKES

HIKES: D, W, L.
TOTAL DISTANCE, W: 16 Miles.
DIFFICULTY: LEVEL II.
SEASON: July 1 — October 1.
USGS MAP: He Devil (1:62,500).
USFS MAP: Hells Canyon-Seven Devils
  Scenic Area (Payette N.F.).
MILEAGE: 161 (17 Dirt).

INTRODUCTION: The west side of the Seven Devils Range, with its precipitous 8,000 foot plunge from He Devil to the Snake River, is scenic and rugged. Sheep Creek is born in six lakes on this west side and then flows north to the Snake. The trail to these lakes, which lie in three distinct cirque basins, is in good Level II condition. It gives several fine views of Hells Canyon and the country beyond.

THE TRAIL: Your goal is Basin Lake, 8 miles in. Day-hikers may hike 3 miles to a scenic divide. The trail starts off to the right of a nice new outhouse. It descends by excellent switchbacks to the East Fork Sheep Creek, from which it climbs to the divide between the East and West Forks. From here, the day-hiker's goal, there is a sweeping view of Hells Canyon and the upper Sheep Creek drainage. Again the trail descends by switchbacks, at last passing under the Devil's Tooth. It crosses the West Fork Sheep Creek and then climbs once more.

The climb takes you to Dry Diggins Ridge and a major trail junction by an old fire telephone. You are going toward Sheep Lake, so take the leftmost trail. After ½ mile more you come to the Sheep Lake Trail, which doesn't appear on your USGS map. Turn left and follow the trail to Basin Lake, which has many campsites.

Shelf Lake is ½ mile farther, requires more climbing, and also has many campsites.

EXTENSIONS: You may continue up the Sheep Lake Trail past Gem Lake to Sheep Lake, which has a good view but very few campsites. You may also explore the area of Bernard Lake and Dry Diggins Ridge and Lookout. Or you can go south past Little Granite and Granite creeks (which drain lakes) and return via the Boise Trail, or just exit at Black Lake.

ACCESS: Same as the Boise Trail (page 93).

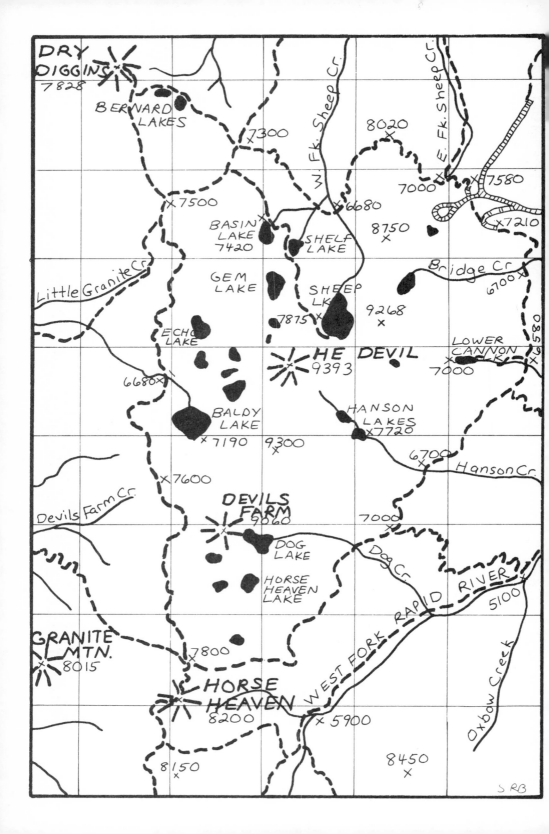

Sheep Creek Lakes — He Devil Mountain

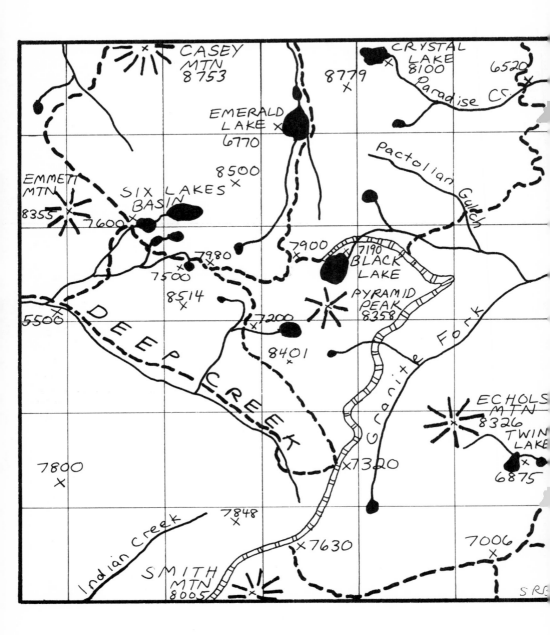

CASEY MTN 8753

CRYSTAL LAKE 8100

×8779

6520

Paradise Cr.

EMERALD LAKE 6770

Pactolian Gulch

8500 ×

EMMETT MTN 8355 ×

SIX LAKES BASIN

7600 ×

7900

7190

BLACK LAKE

7980 ×

7500

8514 ×

×7200

PYRAMID PEAK 8358

Granite Fork

8401 +

ECHOLS MTN 8326

TWIN LAKE 6875

5500 ×

D E E P

C R E E K

7800 ×

×7320

Indian Creek

7848 ×

×7630

7006 ×

SMITH MTN 8005

S.R.

SIX LAKES BASIN

HIKES: D, O, W, L.
TOTAL DISTANCE, W: 15 Miles.
DIFFICULTY: Level II.
SEASON: July 10 — September 27.
USGS MAP: Cuprum (1:62,500).
USFS MAPS: Hells Canyon-Seven Devils
   Scenic Area (Payette N.F.), or Council
   Ranger District (Payette N.F.).
MILEAGE: 177 (33 Dirt).

INTRODUCTION: This is the southern end of the Seven Devils Range. While the mountains here are not so wildly scenic as those in the northern part of the range, they offer outstanding views across Hells Canyon toward the Wallowas. The trails, generally easy to follow and not so steep as those to the north, are Level II.

THE TRAIL: Your goal is any of the Six Lakes, all of which have campsites nearby. The closest lake is 6 miles in, the farthest 7½ miles. Day-hikers and overnighters may stop at Horse Pasture Basin, 4 miles in. The trail from Saddle Camp does not show on your USGS map. It basically contours along the south side of the 8,404-foot peak and gives good opportunities for map and compass work. It then cuts north into Horse Pasture Basin. The only tricky spot is at the first established campsite you reach. The trail goes to the right of a pair of blazed trees and then crosses a stream. More climbing brings you to open country, where there are campsites. From here Joe's Gap is readily visible — which is a good thing, since the trail to the Gap isn't. You will meet the trail from Black Lake at the Gap, and then descend to the first lake via some nice switchbacks.

As you descend from the first lake you cross its outlet creek. The next creek you come to drains the middle two lakes. The trail continues straight from here to a superb view of the Deep Creek valley and to the last and largest lakes.

EXTENSIONS: One simple loop would go down the Lake Creek Trail to the Deep Creek Trail and follow it up to Saddle Camp. A longer loop would continue past the last lakes to Oxbow and Granite Creeks and return via Emerald Lake and Purgatory Saddle.

ACCESS: Take I-84 west from Meridian Road to US-95 near Payette. Drive north to the center of Council. When US-95 turns right you must turn left, on the Hornet Creek Road. Follow signs for Bear and Cuprum until you come to Bear Junction, 31 miles up the road. Go straight for 5 miles, passing through Bear, and turn left on the Black Lake Road. This road is often rough and muddy and may present problems for some vehicles. At the Old Mail Cabin site turn right and follow the Black Lake Road for about 7 miles. The trailhead is signed and comes just before the road passes through a saddle. The camp here is not very large, but there are other sites east of the road in Lost Basin, just north of Smith Mountain. The first campsite on the trail is in Horse Pasture Basin, 3½ miles from the road.

Fourth of July snow at Six Lakes Basin

Area Four
LOWMAN TO LANDMARK

Once the wilderness issue is settled for the "rock and ice" areas of the White Cloud, Pioneer, Lost River, and Lick Creek mountain ranges it will have to re-focus on areas like that from Lowman to Landmark — areas that are not intensive wilderness composed of glaciated peaks, rocky valleys, and scenic lakes, but rather are extensive wilderness consisting of broad ridges, timbered slopes, and pristine streams. Much of Idaho batholith lands from Lowman to Landmark are still roadless — but do they deserve wilderness classification or resource utilization? A look at the variety of hikes presented here, only three of which are currently protected (Elk, Baron, and Pistol lakes), may help answer the question.

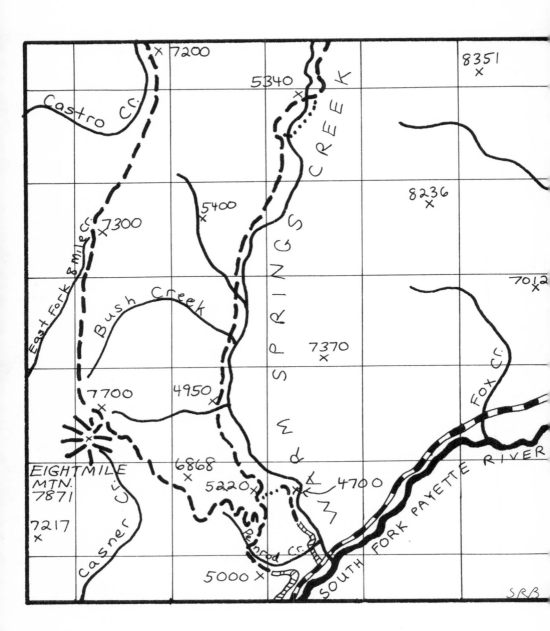

x 7200

8351
x

Castro Cr.

5340
x

5400
x

8236
x

East Fork 8 mile Cr. x 7300

7012
x

Bush Creek

S P R I N G S   C R E E K

7370
x

7700
x

4950
x

Fox Cr.

EIGHTMILE
MTN.
7871

6868
x

5220
x

4700

MEADOW

SOUTH FORK PAYETTE RIVER

7217
x

Casner Cr.

Penrod Cr.

5000 x

SRB

WARM SPRINGS CREEK

HIKES: D, O, W, L.
TOTAL DISTANCE, O: 8 Miles.
DIFFICULTY: Level II.
SEASON: May 20 — October 1.
USGS MAPS: Bull Trout Point, Eightmile
   Mountain.
USFS MAP: Boise N.F.
MILEAGE: 86½ (1½ Dirt).

INTRODUCTION: The present-day Warm Springs Trail follows the Lemhi Trail, an old Indian migration route from the South Fork Payette River to Stanley. It passes through highly erosive headlands which are rich in wildlife, and because of its fine southern exposure it offers good early-season hiking. The best stretches of trail are the first and last 6 miles, which offer scenic hiking and good camping. The center section is 5 miles of winding, climbing, dry trail that stays well above a washed-out stream bed. The Forest Service plans no development in this drainage for the next 20 years. The trail is used by migrating motorcyclists, and the USFS is trying to improve it to minimize damage from them. Level II.

THE TRAIL: Most hikers will start at the Warm Springs Airport trailhead. Those who wish to hike the entire route should start at Bull Trout Lake. From Warm Springs, day-hikers can stop at the canyon view 1½ miles in, while overnighters will find the first campsites after 2½ miles. Weekenders can set up a base camp near the creek that follows Bush Creek, 3½ miles in.

A short climb beside Penrod Creek brings you to a trail divide. Turn right here. After a while you can look down an open slope on Bonneville Hot Springs. A good view up the canyon is not much farther. When the trail ends its descent the campsites begin, and they are nice, grassy ones shaded by ponderosa pine. Such sites continue to the 4-mile mark, the creek past Bush Creek, which you may hike up.

There are very few campsites from here to Castle Creek, a 5-mile stretch of up-down trail that stays above the white scar of the stream bed. The bridge shown on your USGS map ain't there no more! The trail instead stays on the west bank for another ¼ mile and fords the creek in the center of a meadow.

You will probably want to reach the upper part of the trail from the Bull Trout Lake area. (The map for this area is on page 122.) The first 2 miles of trail pass through a mostly level forest that offers unlimited camping. There is one last campsite where you come to the cool waters of Dead Man Creek, and then you descend on trail that will be ruined by continued trail-bike use. When you arrive at the level of Warm Springs Creek the good campsites resume and continue (with interruptions for climbs) to Castle Creek. There are excellent opportunities for high-challenge hiking along upper Warm Springs Creek, No Name Creek, and Cat Creek.

EXTENSIONS: A long loop can be made by hiking up Warm Springs Creek, west on the Kirkham Ridge Trail, and south on the Link Trail (see Eightmile Mountain).

ACCESS: Drive 85 miles on ID-21 from the Boise N.F. ranger station and turn left on the Warm Springs Guard Station/Warm Springs Airport Road. Drive down to the guard station, then right to the end of the airstrip, then left to the trailhead where Penrod Creek enters the meadow. There are a few campsites by the airstrip and the guard station and many more in Forest Service campgrounds along the Payette. The first campsites on the trail are 2½ miles in.

For the Bull Trout Lake trailhead, drive 100 miles from the ranger station on

ID-21, and turn left. Drive 1¾ miles to the trailhead. There are many campsites along the trail and several campgrounds along the road.

Day-hikers' view of Warm Springs Creek

ELK LAKE

HIKES: D, O, W, L.
TOTAL DISTANCE, W: 22 Miles.
DIFFICULTY: Level I.
SEASON: May 15 — October 1.
USGS MAPS: Grandjean*, Edaho Mountain, Warbonnet.
USFS MAP: Sawtooth Wilderness Area (Sawtooth N.R.A.).
MILEAGE: 94 (7 Dirt).

INTRODUCTION: In its course from Grandjean to Elk Lake, the South Fork Payette River shows a changeable nature, and it forces the trail that parallels it to conform to its moods. While the river meanders through Big Meadows, there is enough room for a trail and a road. When it starts to climb above Taylor Springs, the trail gains altitude at a moderate pace. When the South Fork forms a gorge at Fern Falls, the trail is pinched right next to the thundering waters. One more climb for river and trail leads to Elk Lake, not a tarn surrounded by a cirque but a shallow resting place for the river — a pause between the rush from its headwaters and the crash of its great falls. This trail is a major Sawtooth artery, designed and groomed to high standards — Level I.

THE TRAIL: Weekenders should make their goal a campsite between Fern Falls and Elk Lake (11 miles in). Day-hikers may hike 2½ miles to the Goat Creek Falls, while overnighters can find campsites almost anywhere for the first six miles, while a road parallels the trail. You may find snow near Elk Lake as late as June 5. (See the map on page 128 for the first part of this hike.)

Start at the Trail Creek Trail sign and hike across a bridge. The Trail Creek Lakes are 5 hard miles to the left, but you want to go straight. There are good campsites along the river as you hike the long mile to Baron Creek. The lakes at the head of this creek are covered on page 127. One more mile brings you to Goat Creek. There are campsites before and after the bridge and a series of falls a short way up the creek. To reach the falls, climb on the north side of the stream.

Past Goat Creek you have the option of hiking on the trail or on the road below it. The road stays closer to the river and passes many campsites as well as Deadman's Cabin, a miner's grave. The trail stays high and dry. At Taylor Spring the two routes meet and then separate again. The road continues and finally peters out near more campsites. A primitive trail connects it with the main trail at the top of a stream bank that is high above the river.

There are few campsites from here to the camping areas just below Fern Falls and just before Elk Lake. The trail climbs at a very reasonable pace, resorting to gentle switchbacks when necessary. It passes next to Fern Falls, whose crashing din in the spring contrasts strongly with its delicate beauty in the fall. There are only a few campsites at Elk Lake.

EXTENSIONS: The South Fork Trail and its branches lead to many lakes and then pass over into the Middle Fork Boise, Big Queens, and Salmon River drainages.

ACCESS: Take ID-21 from the Boise N.F. ranger station for 87 miles and turn right at the Grandjean sign. Take this dirt road past the lodge to the campgrounds, where you can go straight to the Trail Creek Trail sign or left to the corrals area.

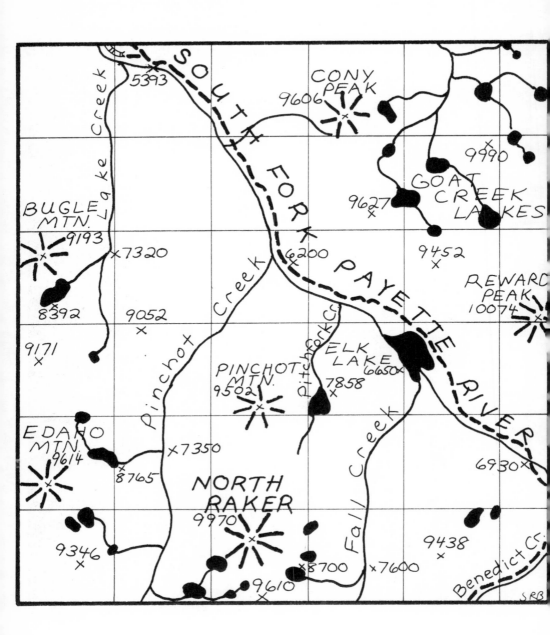

106

Fern Falls — Elk Lake

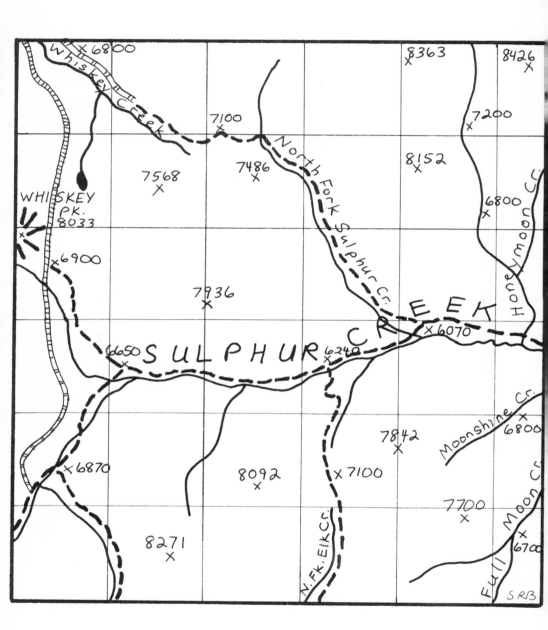

SULPHUR CREEK

HIKES: D, O, W, L.
TOTAL DISTANCE, W: 12 Miles.
DIFFICULTY: Level II.
SEASON: June 25 — October 1.
USGS MAPS: Chinook Mountin, Warm
   Lake (Both 1:62,500).
USFS MAP: Boise N.F.
MILEAGE: 118 (20 Dirt).

INTRODUCTION: Sulphur Creek is a major tributary of the Middle Fork Salmon River and an important salmon-spawning stream. The second half of the hike has been included in the RNRWA, a compromise between environmentalists, who cherish Sulphur Creek's water quality and wildlife habitat, and the Forest Service, which wants to run the proposed Cascade-Stanley Forest Highway across Sulphur Creek's headwaters. Much of the creek valley is broad with gentle gradients, and there are many fine campsites along the Level II trail.

THE TRAIL: Your goal is the junction of the North Fork with main Sulphur Creek, about 6 miles in. Day-hikers and overnighters can stop after 2 miles. To start, cross the meadow at the trail sign and find the trail at the edge of the trees. Turn right and descend alongside the pristine headwaters of Sulphur Creek. The trail leaves the creek and climbs to the left at a bog. It then descends to the junction with a little-used side trail, the day-hikers goal. The fine campsites just past here are the overnighter's goal. There are scattered campsites from here to the North Fork. Once you cross that creek the valley levels out and sites abound.

EXTENSIONS: You may continue on to the Middle Fork of the Salmon and emerge at the Dagger Falls trailhead. However, beyond the Sulphur Creek Lodge the trail becomes a road. You could attempt to locate the two trails your USGS map shows heading south from Sulphur Creek to the North Fork Elk Creek.

You can also make a partial loop by hiking the delightful North Fork Sulphur Creek Trail. The start of the trail is signed on the Landmark-Deadwood Road, ¼ mile north of the South Fork Sulphur Creek Road. The trail starts as a road that bogs down after ¾ mile. It proceeds across meadow, becoming trail as it enters the trees, and then begins a gradual climb to a broad summit. The North Fork is just a short descent from here, and it features cool waters.

ACCESS: Drive 72 miles north from Scenic Junction on ID-55 and turn right on the Warm Lake Road. Follow signs to Landmark, where you turn right. About 4¼ miles south of Landmark junction, turn left on a road marked South Fork Sulphur Creek (just across the Whiskey Creek bridge). The trailhead is 3 miles up the road. There are campsites all along this road and also in the trees just across the meadow from the trailhead.

Sulphur Creek — looking down to the Middle Fork

TRANQUIL BASIN

HIKES: D, O, W, L.
TOTAL DISTANCE, O: 7 Miles.
DIFFICULTY: Levels I, III.
SEASON: June 15 — October 1.
USGS MAPS: Deadwood Reservoir, Boiling Springs (Both 1:62,500).
USFS MAP: Boise N.F.
MILEAGE: 69 Miles (25 Dirt).

INTRODUCTION: While much of the Middle Fork Payette River drainage has been logged, pockets of high-quality wilderness remain around Peace Rock and along Bull Creek. North of Peace Rock lies Tranquil Basin, a sanctuary where man is an infrequent visitor and solitude is the rule. The basin can be reached the hard way from Silver Creek or the easy way from Deadwood Reservoir. The hard route involves a 2,700-foot climb and a 500-foot descent on very poor (or nonexistent) trails, so it is Level III.

The easier route involves a mere 1,200-foot climb over a Level I trail that demonstrates what "multiple use" can mean. Helicopter logging has been conducted near the trail, which is also used as a sheep driveway. But because the Forest Service land use plan calls for preservation of the trail, the route has neither disappeared beneath logging debris nor had its aesthetic value destroyed by clear-cuts. Judicious thinning and careful slash burning have kept the trail, with its views of Deadwood Reservoir, an enjoyable hiking experience.

THE TRAIL: The hike from the Deadwood Reservoir Peninsula Road is only about 3½ miles long. The trailhead is not signed, but the trail goes almost due north from the clearing along a small open drainage. It leaves the drainage and passes through a flat lodgepole forest, after which it starts to climb. There is water along the trail past the logged area. When you reach the saddle at 6,500 feet, the trail divides. The Tranquil Basin Trail goes down to the right; the Boiling Springs Trail goes up to the left.

You are in Tranquil Basin when the descent from the summit ends. You may continue straight ahead on the blazed trail, which peters out near some beaver ponds. Or you may leave the trail, bearing left, and find an old bridge across Basin Creek. There are many campsites in the lodgepole flats.

If you believe you are in good physical condition and wish to find out just how tough you are, hike to Tranquil Basin from Silver Creek over the Devil's Slide Trail. In just over a mile this route gains 2,000 vertical feet — and does it without a switchback! When you are at last overlooking Tranquil Basin, the battle has just begun, for the trail down seems to have disappeared. Yet the rewards are great once you are down in the northwest part of Tranquil Basin, one of the state's wildest places.

The crossing of Silver Creek, near the trail sign, is poorly blazed, but the trail is easy to find once you are on the other side. It climbs gently through a ponderosa pine forest to a small creek, where you should fill canteens. Here the trail turns from angelic to demonic — here begins the Devil's Slide! All ye meek and feeble day-hikers, stop!! Intrepid backpackers, engage low gear and climb! Forget your notions of a two-mile-per-hour pace and hope for 1,000 vertical feet per hour on this stretch. At one point you may hear a small tributary of Ucal Creek to the left of the trail, where you can get water. After you catch up with the ridge, the climb moderates, and at last you come to a well-signed trail junction and a magnificent view.

Turn left here and descend to a saddle between Ucon (or Ucal) and Tranquil basins. A trail sign near a campsite forces you to decide between the two basins.

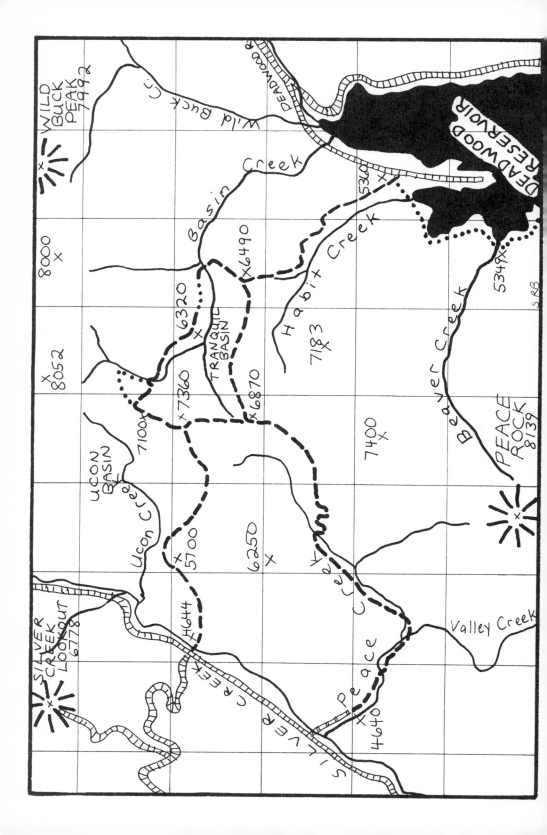

The half-mile to Ucon may seem attractive to you after climbing up the Devil's Slide and reading about the "trail" down to Tranquil Basin, which is very hard to find between the 6,400-foot level in Tranquil Basin and the ridge. Two routes down start at the nortn end of the saddle. You may either contour east along the open ridge, losing altitude at your whim until you come to upper Basin Creek, or you may follow the map route, which descends just on the north side of the drainage that leaves the saddle. Once you reach the trail in the northwest corner of Tranquil Basin, erect a small rock cairn to mark your route back (or you'll get lost just like the author did!). There are two sets of blazes on upper Basin Creek, neither of which seems to lead anywhere. There are many campsites in this part of the basin.

On your return you should use the Peace Creek Trail, since the Devil's Slide is so steep as to be hazardous on the descent. This trail is in better condition and offers different vistas. Take a left at the well-signed trail junction on top of the ridge and hike a mile to a saddle and another divide. The obvious trail goes left to Deadwood Reservoir (the last half of this route is the easy way to Tranquil Basin). Your route out does a disappearing act as it goes to the right, contouring and climbing a bit on the west side of the ridge. It becomes easier to follow as it begins its big descent to Peace Creek and of-fers a view of Peace Rock. There are campsites along Peace Creek, with an especially nice one where you meet the Peace Creek Road — which is ½ mile from the Silver Creek Road, where you are 1½ miles south of the Devil's Slide trailhead.

EXTENSIONS: The large trailless area that surrounds Peace Rock offers more high-challenge hiking.

ACCESS: For the Devil's Slide Trail, drive 34½ miles north on ID-55 from Scenic Junction and turn right on the Garden Valley Road. After 8½ miles turn left on the paved road to Crouch. Turn left just past the cafe in Crouch and continue 15 miles to the Silver Creek Road junction, where you turn right. The Peace Creek Road turns right after 9 miles. The Devil's Slide trailhead is signed and is just past Silver Creek Guard Station, 1½ miles farther. There are campsites along the road and just across Silver Creek.

For the Deadwood Reservoir approach, drive to Landmark via ID-55 and Warm Lake. The new Deadwood Peninsula Road, 24 miles south of Landmark Junction and 6 miles south of the Elk Creek Road, is not yet signed. Neither is the trailhead, 2¼ miles in. This road may be closed in early September to protect wild-life — check with the Forest Service in Lowman for its current status.

Spring in Tranquil Basin

114

EIGHTMILE MOUNTAIN

HIKES: D, O, W, L.
TOTAL DISTANCE, W: 13 Miles.
DIFFICULTY: Level II.
SEASON: June 15 — October 1.
USGS MAP: Eightmile Mountain.
USFS MAP: Boise N.F.
MILEAGE: 86½ (1½ Dirt).

INTRODUCTION: A large roadless area extends north of the South Fork Payette River's course from Lowman to Grandjean. It is an area of creeks and ridges and trails. The Link Trail from Warm Springs Airstrip to Red Mountain is one of the area's finest ridgeline hikes, wandering across forested tablelands, beside beautiful creeks, and along narrow saddles with precipitous dropoffs to either side. It offers excellent views of the surrounding mountains and valleys. While the hike starts with a steep and sometimes rocky climb, the trail is easy to follow, so it is Level II.

THE TRAIL: Weekenders may camp by the East Fork Eightmile Creek, 6½ miles in. Day-hikers and overnighters can hike to the level area at 6,600 feet or the summit at 6,868, about 2 miles in and 1,600 feet up. Fill your canteens as you cross Penrod Creek just past the trailhead. (The next sure water source is a spring at the source of Casner Creek, 4 miles farther.) You soon reach a trail divide, where you turn left. The trail quickly starts climbing and doesn't stop until it reaches the saddle between 6,868 and 6,963 feet. You may camp here or along the open ridge to the right, where there are fine views of the Sawtooths.

The trail now proceeds along the west side of 6,868, not the east side as the USGS map shows. It descends to another saddle and then begins its climb again. A "Sids Point" sign indicates the summit, a nice place to eat breakfast if you camp on the ridge to the right of the trail.

From here to the East Fork Trail sign you lose your southern exposure, and you can encounter snow beyond June 15. You may set up a dry camp in numerous flat areas along the ridge. The only reliable water is in the East Fork. A sign indicates where this abandoned but still easy-to-follow trail branches off to the left. The large level area around this sign is the weekender's goal.

EXTENSIONS: There are no campsites for the next 2 miles of trail, to the crossing of Castro Creek. From there the trail climbs to the northeast flank of 8,391, an area with several good dry campsites. After crossing one last saddle it begins a gradual descent to the Kirkham Ridge Trail. From there a left turn will take you to the Eightmile Creek Trail and the Clear Creek Road (passing the Red Mountain area); a right will take you to Bull Trout Lake, from which you may use the Warm Springs Trail to return to your original trailhead.

ACCESS: Same as the Warm Springs Trail, page 103.

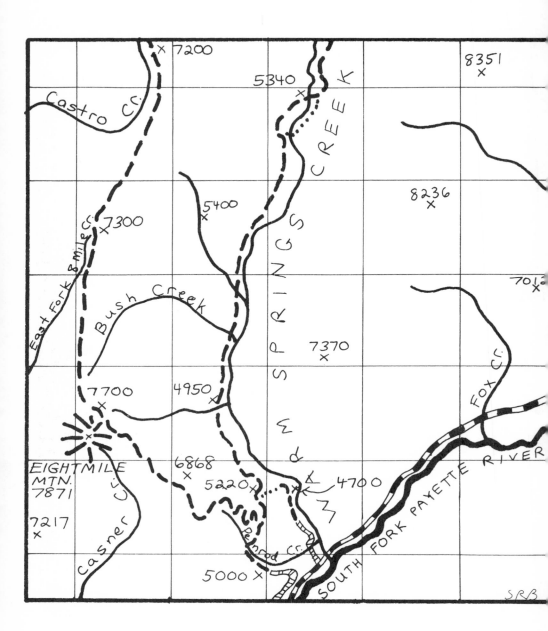

Castro Cr.

×7200

5340
×

SPRINGS CREEK

8351
×

8236
×

×5400

East Fork 8 mile Cr.

×7300

Bush Creek

701⁰
×

7370
×

7700
×

4950
×

Fox Cr.

EIGHTMILE
MTN.
7871

6868
×

5220 ×

4700

SOUTH FORK PAYETTE RIVER

7217
×

Casner Cr.

Penrod Cr.

5000 ×

SRB

116

Rainy day ridgeline hiking at Eightmile Mountain

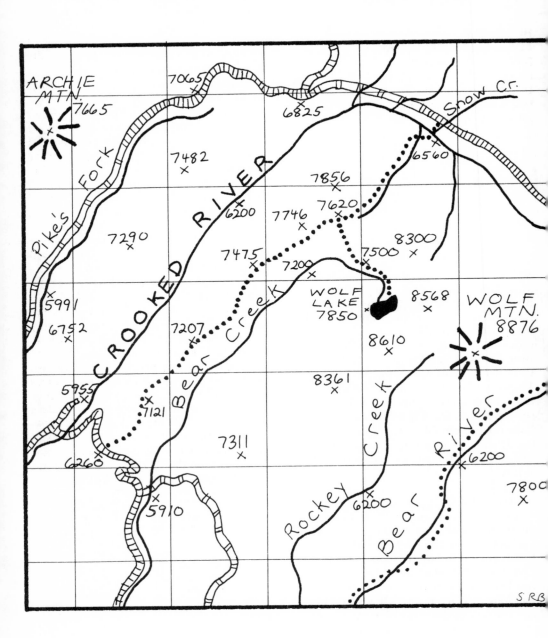

ARCHIE
MTN.
7665

7665
×

Pike's Fork

7065
×

6825
×

Snow Cr.

6560
×

CROOKED RIVER

7482
×

7856
×

7620
×

8300
×

7290
×

6200
×

7746
×

7500
×

7475
×

7200
×

WOLF
LAKE
7850

8568
×

WOLF
MTN.
8876

8876
×

5991
×

6752
×

7207
×

Bear Creek

8610
×

5955
×

7121
×

8361
×

Wolf Creek

Bear River

6260
×

7311
×

6200
×

6200
×

7800
×

5910
×

Rockey Creek

S·R·B

WOLF LAKE

HIKES: O, W.
TOTAL DISTANCE, O: 9 Miles.
DIFFICULTY: Level III.
SEASON: July 4 — October 1.
USGS MAP: Jackson Peak.
USFS MAP: Boise N.F.
MILEAGE: 68 (16½ Dirt).

INTRODUCTION: The Tenmile Creek region, of which the Wolf Mountain-Goat Mountain area is a part, emerged from the RARE II study with a "further planning" recommendation. On the south side of the road to Graham, the names of the area's peaks and streams evoke its wild nature: Bear Creek, Goat Mountain, Cub Creek, Bear River, Wolf Mountain, Snow Creek, Trapper Flat. There are no maintained trails in this area, only a few blazed by sheepherders. One of these leads to Wolf Lake (unaccountably called Jenny Lake by the USGS). It is a rough Level III hike that demands the utmost in route-finding ability.

THE TRAIL: Overnighters and weekenders can reach Wolf Lake, 4½ miles in. Day-hikers might be better off hiking to one of the lakes on either side of the Graham Road, leaving from Silver Creek Summit. Start by walking south on the left side of Snow Creek. As you do, you look directly at the valley you will ascend. Cross to the right of Snow Creek as you approach Crooked River. Try to cross on a big logjam. From here go straight into the woods. After crossing two short boggy stretches you should pick up a faint trail that moves to the right and crosses the creek. Past the crossing the forest opens up, and the trail cuts left and climbs.

When it comes to a bulging ridgelet it cuts right and begins a steep climb to a meadow alongside the creek. The trail probably stays to the right of the creek all the way to the divide with Bear Creek. However, the author always gets impatient with the faint trail and climbs straight up an open slope to the right. He then follows the ridge south to the saddle.

Once you are looking down on upper Bear Creek you can plot your own descent to it. There are campsites in the trees along the creek and also by the lake. The route to the lake stays on the left bank of the creek. You can reach a view of rugged Wolf Mountain by climbing from the lake.

ACCESS: The road to Graham is in poor condition, with steep rocky stretches and numerous blind curves. It needs to be either closed down or fixed up, a fact the Forest Service is painfully aware of. It is usually graded once each year around the Fourth of July and gets progressively worse from then on. Drive 50½ miles from the Boise N.F. ranger station on ID-21 to the Crooked River Road, where you turn right. After 4¼ miles turn left on the Pikes Fork Road (to Graham). After 1¼ miles bear right and tighten your seat belt a notch or two. Past the Jackson Peak Lookout Road the road descends to Crooked River. Snow Creek is signed and comes 1½ miles from the lookout road. There are many campsites here in Trapper Flat.

Wolf Mountain Lake — sunset on the ridge

RED MOUNTAIN LAKES

HIKES: D, O, W, L.
TOTAL DISTANCE, O: 7 Miles.
DIFFICULTY: Level III.
SEASON: June 25 — October 1.
USGS MAPS: Cache Creek, Miller Mountain East.
USFS MAP: Boise N.F.
MILEAGE: 84 (17 Dirt).

INTRODUCTION: Red Mountain anchors the western end of the Warm Springs-Eightmile roadless area. The mountain is surrounded by the Cat, Lost, and Red Mountain lakes, which offer trailless hiking and fishing. A primitive trail offers Level III access to the lakes.

THE TRAIL: Day-hikers may hike to the lookout, 2½ miles, or to the upper lakes, 3½ miles in. Overnighters can make the upper lakes their goal, while weekenders have time to reach the Cat Lakes, 4½ miles in. Fill your canteen as you cross Rough Creek, just past the trailhead. The 1,000-foot climb to the next water can be a dry one.

Just after the lookout comes into view, the trail that leads to it also appears. Climbing to the left, it passes a good spring on the way to the summit. The view from the top embraces the lakes below and the Sawtooths beyond. Be sure to visit the fancy outhouse.

The route to the lakes continues on a fairly level course from the lookout trail divide. There are campsites in the woods before and after you cross a small stream. Just past the stream is a trail divide. The Miller Mountain Trail leads right, and the Kirkham Ridge Trail goes straight, descending to some other lakes and to campsites at Eightmile Creek. The route to the

Red Mountain Lakes climbs left from the divide on an open ridge. To reach the lower lake and the Cat Lakes, contour on the right side of the ridge after you have climbed a while. You will reach a lake that is in the Clear Creek drainage. A climb to the left of this lake takes you over a boulder-strewn divide to the lower lake, where there is little camping. There are more campsites at the first Cat Lake, an easy walk from the lower lake.

To reach the upper lakes, continue up the open ridge. When the ridge narrows and becomes more treed, you can look over the side and pick a route down to the lake at 8,106 feet. There are campsites below this lake and also along the route to the lake at 8,262. You might exit the lakes area by way of the lookout. The best route up leaves the 8,262-foot lake.

EXTENSIONS: You may continue on the Kirkham Ridge Trail to Bull Trout Lake and complete the Warm Springs Creek-Link Trail loop. Or you may lose yourself in the Lost Lakes.

ACCESS: Drive to Lowman Junction, 66¼ miles from the Boise N.F. ranger station on ID-21. Take a soft left here on the Clear Creek Road. Drive 12 miles up this road to the Red Mountain Lookout Road, where you turn right. There are campsites along this road, which ends at the trailhead. The first campsites along the trail are 2 miles in, near the stream. This road is often closed during the week for logging traffic. The Lowman Ranger Station can give you current information on road closures.

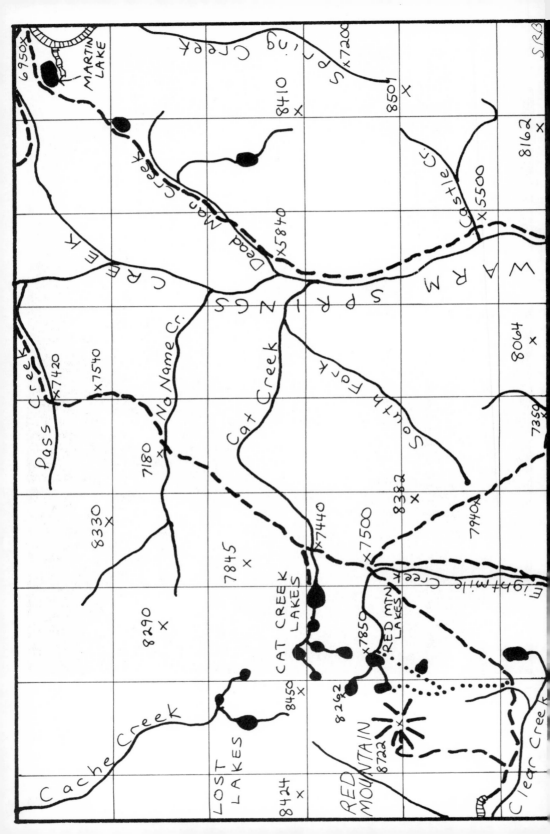

Aerial view of Red Mountain Lakes

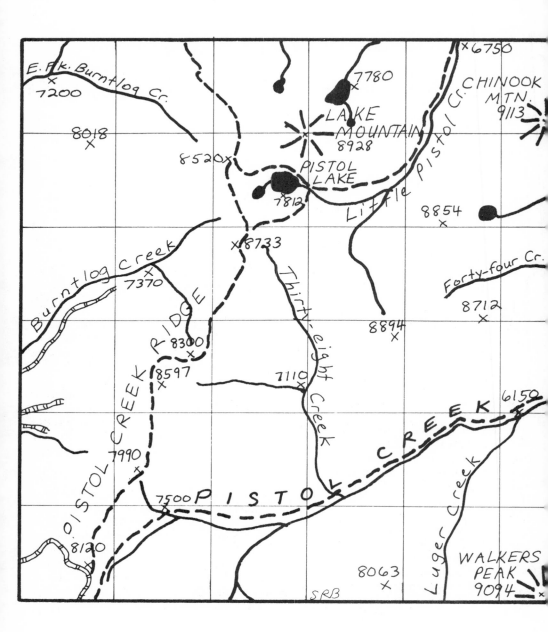

E. Fk. Burntlog Cr.
x 7200

8018 x

8520 x

x 6750

7780 x

LAKE MOUNTAIN
8928

CHINOOK MTN.
9113

PISTOL LAKE

7812

Little Pistol Cr.

8854 x

Burntlog Creek

x 7370

PISTOL CREEK RIDGE

8300 x

8597 x

x 8733

Thirty-eight Creek

7110 x

Forty-four Cr.

8712 x

8894 x

6150

PISTOL CREEK

7990

7500

PISTOL

CREEK

Luger Creek

8120

8063 x

SRB

WALKERS PEAK
9094 x

124

PISTOL LAKE

HIKES: D, O, W, L.
TOTAL DISTANCE, W: 11 Miles.
DIFFICULTY: Level II.
SEASON: July 4 — September 13.
USGS MAP: Chinook Mountain (1:62,500).
USFS MAP: Boise N.F.
MILEAGE: 116 (7 Dirt).

INTRODUCTION: The hike to Pistol Lake, in the southwest corner of the River of No Return Wilderness Area, will introduce you to one of the RNRWA's great glories — ridgeline hiking. The wilderness area has many similar ridgeline trails. While the lake itself is primitive, the area just west of it has been logged, and the ridge just south of Pistol Creek has been roaded. You will use this Artillery Dome Road to reach the trailhead. From there the road heads southeast, with much of its route inside the wilderness boundary. This is a typical conflicting use of the RNRWA and for the usual reason — mining. Most of this trail is Level II, but the final descent to the lake is a hectic Level III plunge.

THE TRAIL: The weekender's goal is Pistol Lake, 5½ miles in. Day-hikers may stop at the view above the switchbacks. Overnighters unable to reach the lake can settle for a dry ridgeline campsite above it.

The trail stays on the ridgetop for a mile past the trail sign, passing good dry campsites along the way. It then descends to the first saddle. It is a wet one, and you can find water down the drainage to the right. From here you climb via switchback to the west side of the ridge and a fine view, the day-hiker's goal.

You suddenly come to the end of the

ridge and a view of Burntlog Creek. The trail cuts right and descends along a steep northern exposure that can easily hold snow through July. There are some campsites around the saddle that follows and a spring a little farther down the trail. From the spring you climb to 8,733 feet and a trail divide.

From the trail sign you look down on the two Pistol Lakes. There are two routes down. The trail that leaves this divide doesn't show on the USGS map. It goes down a side ridge toward 8,699 feet, cuts left to the more level area due south of the lower lake, and then makes a nasty descent of the last 500 feet. The other trail, which shows on both maps, is longer and just as steep, but it gives better access to the upper lake.

The obvious campsites are at the outlet of Pistol Lake, but dry campsites offer a chance to avoid carrying your pack on the nasty final stretch. Such campsites can be found on the ridge overlooking the lake or on the more level area above the big plunge. You might also try the upper lake or the meadow southeast of it.

EXTENSIONS: You may hike the entire River of No Return Wilderness Area from here. One good loop would go down Little Pistol Creek and up Pistol Creek to your car. Or you could continue north on the ridgeline trail.

ACCESS: Drive 72 miles north of Scenic Junction on ID-55 to the Warm Lake Road. Turn right and drive to Landmark. Turn right at Landmark junction, go a short ¼ mile on the Deadwood Road, and then turn left on the Artillery Dome Road. After 1¾ miles bear left, and after 2 more miles the Artillery Dome Road turns right. Passenger cars can probably go just 1¼ miles of the 3 miles to the trailhead. There are campsites all along this road and a short distance down the trail.

Pistol Lake — Primitive Area ridgeline hiking (Center Mountain Trail)

BARON LAKES

HIKES: D, W, L.
TOTAL DISTANCE, W: 21 Miles.
DIFFICULTY: Level II.
SEASON: July 4 — October 1.
USGS MAPS: Grandjean*, Stanley Lake*,
   Warbonnet Peak.
USFS MAP: Sawtooth Wilderness Area
   (Sawtooth N.R.A.).
MILEAGE: 94 (7 Dirt).

INTRODUCTION: When you go to Baron you go to the heart of the Sawtooths. The many summits around you, composed of the pink rock of the Sawtooth batholith, face west and turn orange in the sun's last rays. Although there is one steep, rocky stretch, overall the hike is rated Level II.

THE TRAIL: Your goal is Baron Lake, 10½ miles in and 3,100 feet up. Day-hikers and overnighters can reach the forks of Baron Creek, 3 miles in. The mile from the trailhead to the Baron Creek Trail, where you turn left, is a long one. There are campsites along the river to the right of this stretch. There are few campsites along Baron Creek until you approach the forks and a trail divide, where there are several.

Bear right from the divide for the Baron Lakes and steadily climb. There are a few campsites in the mile past Moolack Creek. As you continue upcanyon the view is dominated by three hanging valleys and the waterfalls that drain them: Tohobit, Warbonnet, and Baron Creek falls. If you want to become a member of the exclusive club of Baron Lake visitors you must pay the dues and make the 1,000-foot climb to the left of the falls. Once above them the trail meanders up, down, around, and across Baron Creek, passing some camping areas along the way.

If you turn right at the second bridge and climb on the right side of the small creek, you will come to some campsites by a pool that reflects the heights above. More climbing brings you to some good campsites on a moraine north of Little Baron Creek.

If you continue on the main trail you pass several parks — level areas that make good campsites. Since camping at Baron Lake itself is limited, these sites are good alternatives. The parks continue to just 100 yards from the lake. At Baron Lake you can camp at the campground east of the outlet (complete with outhouse). There are very few campsites along the northwest shore of the lake and none at all at Upper Baron Lake.

EXTENSIONS: The only trail out of the Baron Lakes climbs to Baron Summit, where you have an excellent view to the south, looking up Redfish Lake Creek. A loop hike would travel past Cramer and Hidden lakes to the headwaters of the South Fork Payette River and go down the river to Grandjean via Elk Lake

ACCESS: Same as Elk Lake (page 105).

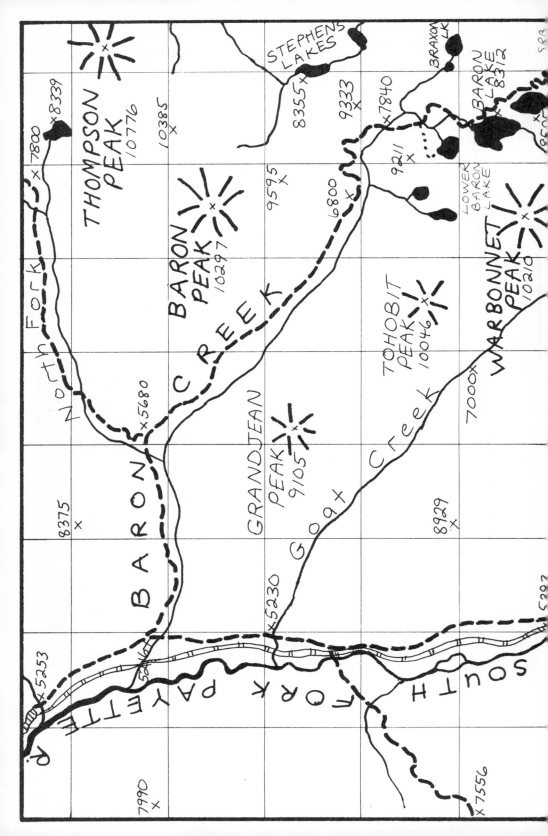

Baron Lake — the heart of the Sawtooths

Area Five
AROUND STANLEY

The Sawtooth Valley, with the Stanley Basin anchoring its northern end, is surely one of the nation's most beautiful spots. It is surrounded by mountains — the Sawtooths to the west, the White Clouds to the east, the Salmon River Range peaks to the north, and the Smokies and Boulders to the south. A myriad of trails, suitable for hikers of all abilities, leaves the area. Many of these trails lead to fragile alpine lake and meadow areas which are quickly degraded by heavy human use. Campfires have already been banned in the most congested places, and a restrictive system may be necessary to protect them even more.

There are great contrasts between the mountains to the east and the west of Stanley. The White Clouds, to the east, are composed mainly of sedimentary rocks. The Sawtooths, to the west, are made of igneous rock. The White Cloud trail system is generally atrocious, with an absolute minimum of switchbacks and (seemingly) an absolute maximum of altitude gains. The Sawtooth trail system is generally excellent, with switchback trails built and rebuilt to the latest standards and with smaller altitude gains. The less-known White Clouds, with tough trails and hard-to-reach trailheads, offer more seclusion. The better-known Sawtooths, easy to reach from US-93, seem to be overrun with rabid hikers much of the summer. The White Clouds, with valuable mineral deposits, have not received wilderness designation. The Sawtooths became a Primitive Area in 1937 and a Wilderness Area in 1972.

Most of the hikes in this section lead to popular mountain lakes. You can minimize your impact on the lakes and on the other people who visit them by carrying your stove, camping at least 100 feet from lakes, and leaving a cleaner camp than you found.

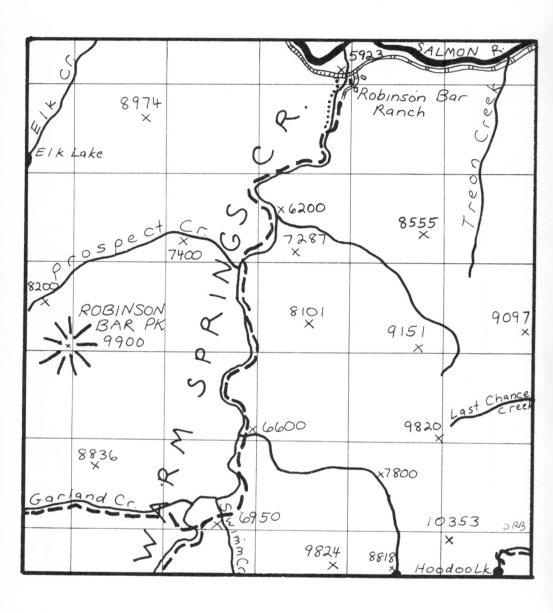

SALMON R.

5923 ×

Robinson Bar
Ranch

Elk Cr.

8974 ×

Elk Lake

Treon Creek

×6200

8555 ×

Prospect Cr.

7400 ×

7287 ×

8200 ×

ROBINSON
BAR PK
9900

8101 ×

9151 ×

9097 ×

WARM SPRINGS CR.

Last Chance Creek

×6600

9820 ×

8836 ×

×7800

Garland Cr.

Swim Cr.

×6950

10353
JRB
×

9824 ×

8818 ×

Hoodoo Lk.

132

WARM SPRINGS CREEK

HIKES: D, O, W, L.
TOTAL DISTANCE, W: 14 Miles.
DIFFICULTY: Level II.
SEASON: June 5 — October 1.
USGS MAP: Robinson Bar.
USFS MAP: White Cloud-Boulder Mountains (Sawtooth N.R.A.).
MILEAGE: 141 (2 Dirt).

INTRODUCTION: Warm Springs Creek is the longest stream in the White Clouds. In its 25-mile course from the Born Lakes under Patterson Peak to the main Salmon at Robinson Bar, it drops some 4,000 feet, and it is always accompanied by a trail. Its lower and upper stretches are closed to trail bikes, and bighorn sheep summer in some of its side canyons. The trailhead has a problem that is typical of White Cloud hiking — it must be reached by crossing private property. The solution here is much simpler than it is at the Champion Creek or the East Fork Salmon River trailheads, for a bypass exists. The very first part of the bypass is Level III, but the rest of the trail is Level II, easy to follow but heavy on the up-down stuff.

THE TRAIL: Your goal is Swimm Creek, about 7 miles in. Overnighters and day-hikers can hike from 1 to 3 miles and enjoy the open, level forests along lower Warm Springs Creek. The bypass trail starts about 100 feet west of the Robinson Bar Ranch gate. It goes up 100 feet and over a finger of ridge, descending to the creek only to climb over another, less steep, ridgelet. The maintained trail and the good campsites begin just after the second descent. One bad stretch comes early, when the trail divides. At low water you can go down to the left and snake along the creek. At high water you must climb to the right to an old canal, from which you quickly descend.

After the trail comes very close to the creek it steeply climbs a stream bank. From here you have a view of the craggy point at 7,287 feet. Not long after your descent from the high bank, the trail forks where it crosses the creek. The left fork goes to a ford, the right fork proceeds for 100 feet and then cuts left to reach the primitive bridge across the creek. After you cross, campsites become fewer, with some of the best ones around an old cabin and along a meandering stretch of Warm Springs Creek.

You will instantly recognize the start of the climb to Swimm Creek — the trail actually has a switchback. There are excellent campsites before and after the creek crossing. You may continue down to the junction with the Garland Creek Trail in a meadow where there is more camping.

EXTENSIONS: If you continue up Warm Springs Creek you have about 6 miles of trail that are open to trail bikes and 9 more closed miles to Born Lakes. You may also climb from the creek to Garland Lakes (via trail) or to Swimm Lake (cross-country).

ACCESS: Drive to Stanley on ID-21 via Lowman, or on I-80, US-20, and ID-75 via Ketchum. Drive 15 miles past Stanley to Robinson Bar Road, then drive past the USFS campgrounds to the Robinson Bar Ranch gate. Park on the right before the gate and hunt for the trailhead. You may camp in the Forest Service campgrounds along the Salmon River or about one mile in on the trail.

Side creek of Warm Springs Creek

WEST FORK
YANKEE FORK

HIKES: D, O, W, L.
TOTAL DISTANCE, W: 12 Miles.
DIFFICULTY: Levels I, II.
SEASON: June 10 — October 1.
USGS MAPS: Mount Jordan, East Basin
 Creek*.
USFS MAP: Challis N.F. (West Half).
MILEAGE: 147 (7 Dirt).

INTRODUCTION: Maps identify this area simply as part of the Salmon River Range, which extends across the River of No Return Wilderness Area all the way to McCall. There are many roadless regions in this range, but this is one of the prettiest. It is dominated by Mount Jordan, Cabin Creek Peak, and the elusive Tango. RARE II passed over this area, which has active mining claims, and its future for hikers is now in doubt. The West Fork of the Yankee Fork of the Salmon River is a gentle stream, and aside from a steep initial climb the trail that follows it is Level I.

THE TRAIL: The weekender's goal is the junction of Cabin Creek and the West Fork, about 5½ miles in. Day-hikers and overnighters can stop at Lightning Creek, 3 miles in. The hike starts with a nasty climb that may make beginners give up the sport. Don't give up! Once you have descended to the West Fork again, the hike becomes a real cakewalk. There are innumerable campsites, beginning at the Deadwood Trail junction. Most of these are in the forest, though meadows before and after the Lightning Creek crossing offer a view of Red Mountain. You will probably have to ford Lightning Creek.

The hike from there to the Cabin Creek Trail goes quickly. At this point you must make a choice. You can set up a base camp here or just up Cabin Creek and then day-hike some of the area's peaks or trails. Or you can camp farther up the West Fork or up Cabin Creek.

The hike further up Cabin Creek is rewarding because of the good campsites, the outstanding views of the head of the drainage, and the possibility of continuing on to the Crimson Lakes. There are more good campsites after the first crossing of Cabin Creek, and the meadows along the trail give excellent views up the valley. Two stretches of the trail are washed out. At the second such stretch you cross the creek again, fording in the middle of a meadow directly across from an avalanche scar on the other side.

More campsites and scenic views are found from here to the third crossing, which marks the end of the level valley. Just past this crossing a well-beaten but unblazed path leads left to a mining camp. (If you are heading for Crimson Lakes, check here to see whether they are blasting.) Bear right at the path, climb a little, and you will come to another trail divide. To the right are Pioneer Creek and Loon Creek Guard Station. To the left is a very rough and steep blazed trail to Crimson Lake, about 2 miles farther. If you hike partway up this trail you will see Red Mountain and Cabin Creek Peak.

EXTENSIONS: One loop would go north past Cabin Creek to Loon Creek, south past Horseshoe Lake to Knapp Creek, and then east past Hindman Lake to the West Fork Yankee Fork. The Lightning Creek Trail also offers good hiking.

ACCESS: Drive to Stanley, 124 miles from the Boise N.F. ranger station on ID-21. Turn left on ID-75 and drive 13 miles to the Sunbeam-Bonanza-Custer Road and turn left again. Drive 8 miles to the Bonanza Guard Station/West Fork Forest Camp Road and turn left. At the three-way divide past the guard station go right, at the two cemetery signs bear left, and then bear left for the West Fork forest camp. About ¼ mile past this fork is a

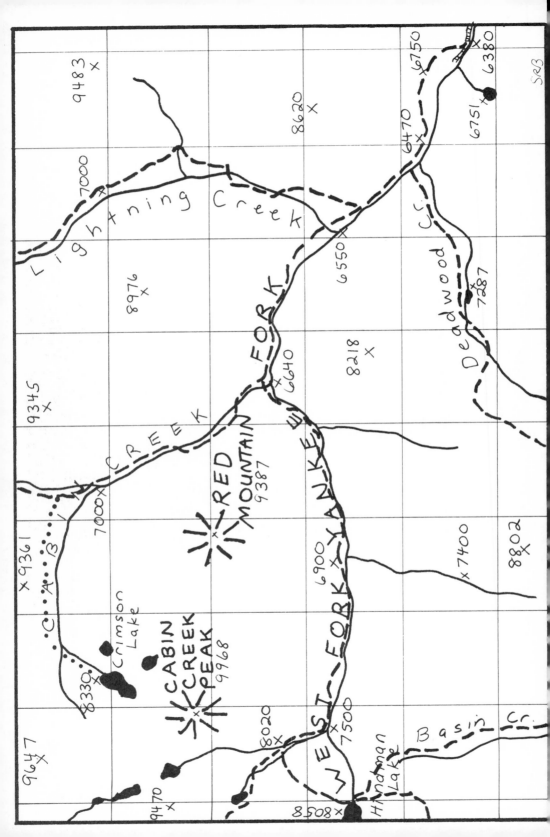

pleasant level area. In rainy, wet weather park (and camp) here, as the road soon takes a very steep dive to the river level and the campground. At the base of the steep descent is a trail sign, which you should ignore if you can reach the campground. There is another trailhead by the campground outhouse.

Red Mountain dominates the West Fork of Yankee Fork.

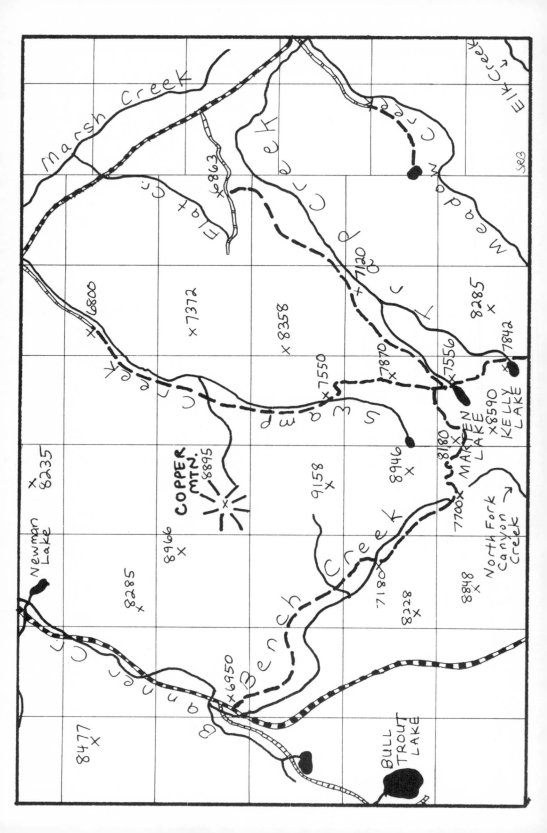

MARTEN LAKE

HIKES: D, O, W, L.
TOTAL DISTANCE, W: 9 to 12 Miles.
DIFFICULTY: Levels I, II.
SEASON: June 25 — October 1.
USGS MAPS: Banner Summit, Elk Meadow.
USFS MAP: West Half Challis N.F.
MILEAGE: 100 (No Dirt).

INTRODUCTION: When the Sawtooth Wilderness Area was created the northern end of the Sawtooth Range was left out, an omission that may soon be remedied. This region includes the upper Elk Creek drainage and several alpine lakes in the Marsh Creek drainage. Because it is outside the designated wilderness, this handsome area has received little use. It is well trailed, with three different routes, two of which are covered here, leading to Marten Lake. The Trap Creek Trail is an easy Level I hike, while the Bench Creek Trail has a steep descent off a summit that makes it Level II.

THE TRAIL: Your goal is Marten Lake, with two more lakes, Kelly and Elizabeth, not far beyond. The lake is 6 miles in by the Bench Creek Trail, 4½ miles in by the Trap Creek Trail. The Bench Creek Trail starts through beautiful open timber on its way to the summit above Marten Lake. It starts on a wide, level trail that makes for very mellow hiking and good dry campsites. At last you come to an overview of the Bench Creek meadows and a Bench Creek sign. Bear left here. The trail generally stays at the foot of a ridge, on the left edge of a particularly mosquito-infested meadow. Along this flat stretch there is water and a spot where the trail loses itself in a meadow. Go straight and a little to the left and you'll find it.

After you cross the second tributary stream (shown on the USGS map) the trail begins to climb, and campsites become scarce. Climb at a moderate rate to the Bench Creek-North Fork Canyon Creek divide, where there is a gigantic Forest Service sign. You must be careful to get on the correct trail here. The Boise N.F. "Land Use Plan for the South Fork Payette River Planning Area" (1975) states: "A trail once existed from the mouth of the North Fork of Canyon Creek to the Bench Creek Trail on the Challis N.F. The trail was eliminated from the maintained system in 1966. Maps prior to this date still show the trail." However, the new (1976) Boise N.F. map shows the trail! (The new West Half Challis N.F. map doesn't.) While the author saw no signs of this trail in the divide area, you should be sure you climb to the left shortly after leaving the saddle.

The trail deteriorates from here to Marten Lake. It is poorly blazed and tricky, switching back from time to time when you least expect it. However, its goal — the high saddle just west of Marten Lake — is clear, and the country is open and easy to travel in. Even if you stray off the trail you should have no trouble reaching the ridge. From the high saddle the trail drops off to the left, not to the right as the map shows. This is a bad stretch, close to Level III, so use caution.

At last you are down and above Marten Lake, passing through an open lodgepole forest with campsites. You then come to junctions with the Swamp Creek and Trap Creek trails, and to Marten Lake. Most of the campsites at Marten are too close to the lakeshore — try to find one farther away. Kelly Lake, which is not far, has few campsites, though the three little lakes (marshes?) to the east may be suitable.

The Trap Creek Trail is not as pretty as the Bench Creek Trail, but it's certainly shorter and easier to follow. It is 4½ miles from the trailhead to the lake, and the total climb is only 600 feet. The trail is dry during its first two miles, passing across an interesting dry lakebed (shown with water on the USGS map) and then by a large marsh. It has up-and-down stretches most of the way to Marten Lake. At one point it descends to a spring in a meadow, which is the last camping area to the lake.

EXTENSIONS: You could go in one trail and out the other, hitchhiking to your car. You could also go on to Elizabeth Lake or all the way to Elk Creek. Upper Elk Creek offers many opportunities for alpine exploration.

ACCESS: The Bench Creek trailhead is 100 miles from the Boise N.F. ranger station on ID-21. To reach the Trap Creek trailhead, go up ID-21 another 11½ miles and turn right on a dirt road (at elevation 6,696). The trail starts a short mile in, but you may have to park at the crossing of the intermittent stream shown on the USGS map. It is a rough crossing, wet or dry. If you use the Bench Creek Trail you can car-camp at Bull Trout Lake or make a trailside camp anywhere in the first 2 miles. If you use the Trap Creek Trail you can camp along the dirt road or in the first ½ mile of trail.

Marten Lake — northern Sawtooth headlands

LANGER LAKES

HIKES: D, O, W.
TOTAL DISTANCE, O: 5 Miles.
DIFFICULTY: Levels I, II.
SEASON: June 30 — October 1.
USGS MAPS: Langer Peak, Cape Horn Lakes.
USFS MAP: West Half Challis N.F.
MILEAGE: 113½ (7½ Dirt).

INTRODUCTION: The Middle Fork Salmon River, one of the West's most renowned white-water runs, is born at the confluence of Marsh and Bear Valley creeks. This stream junction is surrounded by three large mountains: Blue Bunch to the west, Cape Horn to the south, and Ruffneck to the east. At the base of Ruffneck Peak, which has a fire lookout, is a pretty basin with five lakes. It would make an excellent area for beginning backpackers because it is an easy, short hike into an easy-to-stay-found-in area. A gentle Level I trail leads to Langer Lake, and Level II trails lead to the other lakes and the lookout.

THE TRAIL: Your goal is Langer Lake, about 2½ miles in, a short day or overnight hike. The trail begins with a steep stretch exactly where the trailhead sign points and is easy to follow to the lake, which has many campsites around it. You may also want to camp at or near Ruffneck Lake, which is less accessible and has no trail to it but is easy to find. Camping is poor by Island and Rocky lakes, but there are many good nonlake campsites in the basin.

Once you have set up camp, try the 1,400-foot climb to the lookout. The trail ascends to the ridge south of the peak and then cuts right. The view from the top is excellent.

EXTENSIONS: If you go south on the lookout ridge you can connect with trails to Mable Lakes or the Middle Fork Salmon River.

ACCESS: Take ID-21 from the Boise N.F ranger station for 106 miles, to the Seafoam area turnoff. Go left and follow signs for the Seafoam Guard Station, immediately taking a right and then after ½ mile a left. After 7 more miles you will see the Langer Monument and your trailhead. Parking and camping here are problems. You can camp at many spots along the dirt road you took in. There is no camping on the trail to Langer Lake.

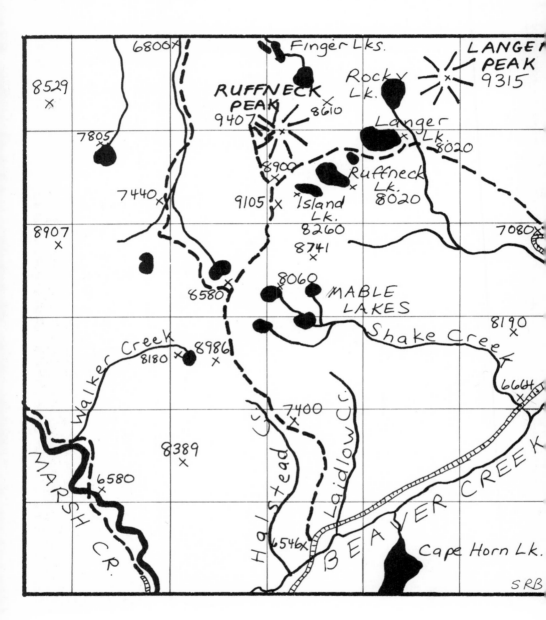

6800 X

Finger Lks.

LANGER
PEAK
9315

8529
X

Rocky
Lk.

RUFFNECK
PEAK
9407
8610

Langer
Lk.
8020

7805
X

8900

Ruffneck
Lk.
8020

7440
X

9105 X

Island
Lk.

8907
X

8260

7080

8741
X

8060

MABLE
LAKES

6580

8190
X

Walker Creek

8986

Shake Creek

8180
X

6664

7400

Laidlow Cr.

8389
X

Halstead Cr.

BEAVER CREEK

MARSH CR.

6580

6546 X

Cape Horn Lk.

SRB

142

Langer Lakes — Ruffneck Peak

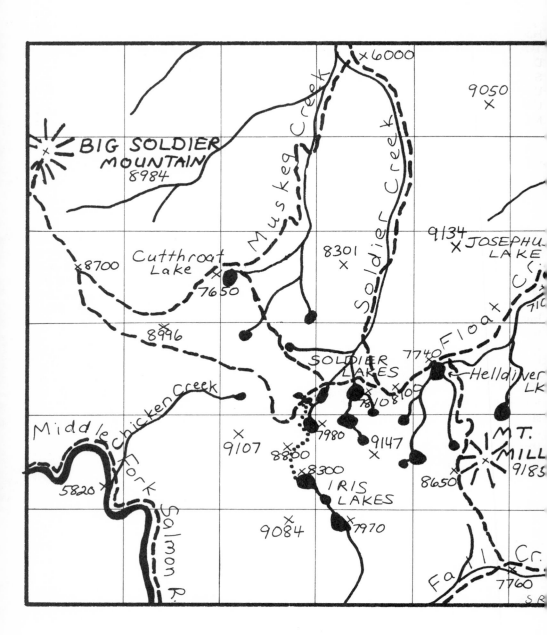

SOLDIER LAKES

HIKES: D, O, W, L.
TOTAL DISTANCE, W: 12 Miles.
DIFFICULTY: Level II.
SEASON: July 4 — September 13.
USGS MAP: Greyhound Ridge (1:62,500).
USFS MAP: West Half Challis N.F.
MILEAGE: 136 (20 Dirt).

INTRODUCTION: The Soldier Lakes have long been one of Idaho's most popular hiking areas. They are highly regarded for mountain and canyon sight-seeing, for high lake fishing, and as a base camp for trail riding along the Middle Fork Salmon River. The Forest Service allowed trail bikers access to the area until 1978, to the detriment of the trail and the lakes. With the Soldier Lakes included in the new River of No Return Wilderness Area, they should recover from the trail-bike invasion and again offer solitude to complement their scenery. While the trail is neither steep nor hard to follow, it will be Level II until it is rebuilt and its washed out sections are replaced.

THE TRAIL: Your goal is whichever of the six Soldier Lakes meets your fancy, beginning with one 6 miles in. Day-hikers and overnighters can stop at Helldiver Lake, 2 miles in. The trail loses no time in climbing from Josephus Lake to Helldiver Lake, where there are a few campsites. The climb from there to the divide is rough and rocky.

After the summit you descend by switchbacks to a level area and a trail divide, where there are some campsites. Turn left at the divide, and soon you will be on a rocky traverse of great beauty, followed shortly by First Lieutenant Lake,

which has campsites. Continue to Colonel Lake if you wish, where there are campsites and a trail divide. The two lakes you have now passed receive heavy pack-stock use. Since horse packers are unable to camp and leave no trace (if you nose what I means), the upper lakes are recommended for camping.

The first upper lake is easily reached from First Lieutenant Lake, the second from the trail divide by Colonel Lake. To reach the second go left from the trail divide to General Lake. Climb left from here on a trail and you will come to an unnamed lake (Unknown Soldier Lake?). There is a spring at the southwest corner of this lake.

This trail continues past the spring in the direction of Iris Lakes, where there is also good camping. The Cutthroat Lakes are only 2 miles from the Colonel Lake trail divide, to the right. Cutthroat and Iris offer safety-valve camping if the Soldier Lakes are crowded.

EXTENSIONS: Both trails from the Colonel Lake divide lead to Big Soldier Lookout and would make an 11-mile loop route. You could also go down past the Cutthroat Lakes to the Middle Fork Salmon River, proceed downstream, and then return by Soldier Creek. (Fords of the river would best be crossed in late season.) Finally, you could hike to Iris Lakes and return by way of the divide west of Mount Mills, using either a ridgeline route or the Fall Creek Trail.

ACCESS: Follow directions given for Langer Lake (page 141) except continue 6½ miles to Seafoam Guard Station. Go straight from there for another 6½ miles to Josephus Lake, the trailhead. (Ignore side roads that lead to mines.) There is a campground at Josephus Lake, but it is very primitive and usually crowded. There are some roadside campsites back down Float Creek Road that may be better. The road into Josephus Lake is narrow and usually rough, so use caution.

Old snag on the ridge at Soldier Lakes

McGOWAN LAKES

HIKES: D, O, W, L.
TOTAL DISTANCE, W: 20 Miles.
DIFFICULTY: Levels I, II.
SEASON: July 4 — October 1.
USGS MAP: Stanley Lake.
USFS MAP: Sawtooth Wilderness Area
  (Sawtooth N.R.A.).
MILEAGE: 123 (4 Dirt).

INTRODUCTION: Mount McGowan is the farthest north of the super-rugged Sawtooth peaks, and Stanley Lake Creek, below it, marks the current Sawtooth Wilderness Area boundary. The McGowan Lakes, south of the peak, are less crowded than most other Stanley Front lakes, and they serve as a base camp for viewing scenic but crowded Sawtooth Lake. The route to the lakes follows an old mining road for seven miles before becoming a good level II trail.

THE TRAIL: Your goal is the McGowan Lakes, 10 miles in. Day-hikers and over-nighters may stop near Bridalveil Falls, 4 miles in. Fill your canteen in the campground, for cattle use the creek for the first 2 miles. A leisurely hike takes you to the Alpine Way Trail junction and a registration box. Go right on the road towards Sawtooth Lake. Climb to avoid Lady Lace Falls and descend to cross Stanley Lake Creek on a very rickety log bridge. There are campsites beyond the crossing and out of the cow zone. Bridalveil Falls is a mile farther.

After the Elk Creek turnoff, 1½ miles past the falls, the road begins to climb and the campsites end. After a steep stretch where the road switchbacks, it proceeds to Greenback Mine. Your trail cuts off to the left toward Trail Creek. It climbs gently to the Trail Creek-Stanley Lake Creek divide, where there is camping.

Take the trail that goes left from the divide, and fill your canteen in the small creek that soon follows. As you climb on this excellent trail you can see Observation and Hanson peaks. The trail crosses a ridge and descends to a marshy area, just beyond which are campsites. The trail climbs and again descends to a basin of lakes and campsites. It goes directly between the twin McGowan Lakes and then climbs to the highest lake, which has few campsites. There are several dry campsites on the trail above the upper lake, reaching all the way to the pass, where you have a breathtaking view of Sawtooth Lake and Mount Regan.

EXTENSIONS: Your very best extension is to complete a 20-mile loop via Sawtooth Lake and the Alpine Way Trail. Descend to Sawtooth Lake, whose few camping areas are often overcrowded. Go left from the trail divide at the outlet. You now enter a world of boring switchbacks that take you past Alpine Lake (which also has few campsites), across Iron Creek, and down to the Alpine Way Trail, where you turn left.

This is a no-frills trail, little used, that has a character all its own. It gives access to some untrammeled parts of the Sawtooths and good views of Stanley Basin and the White Clouds. Dry campsites and wet creeks are scattered along the 6-mile hike to Stanley Lake Creek. The only confusing stretch is the avalanche scar on the North Fork Crooked Creek, where the trail descends a bit. There are many campsites as you approach Stanley Lake Creek, which you can cross on some upstream logs. You must then bear left to return to the registration box.

This loop route could be extended to a week's trip as follows: day 1, Bridalveil Falls; day 2, Hanson Lakes; day 3, traverse to the Elk Creek Trail and descend to Stanley Lake Creek; day 4, McGowan Lakes; day 5, Alpine Lake; day 6, cirque basin east of McGowan Peak by 8,575 pond; day 7, out.

ACCESS: Drive 119 miles from the Boise N.F. ranger station on ID-21 to the Stanley Lake Road (5 miles west of Stanley). Turn right and drive 3¼ miles. Take a left on the Inlet Campground Road, then bear right to Area B, and right again to the trailhead.

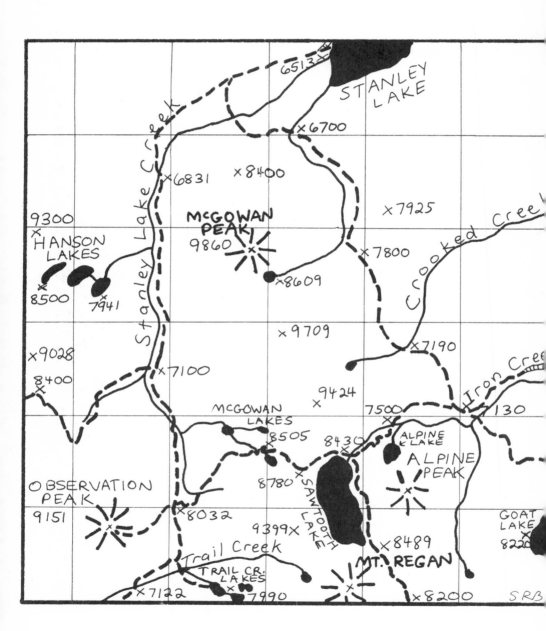

McGowan Lakes — cirque basin below McGowan Peak

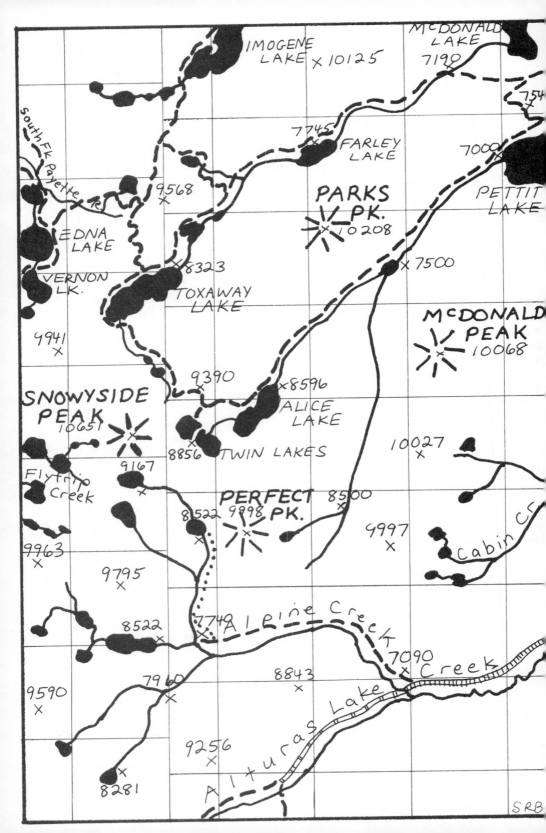

ALICE-TWIN-TOXAWAY LOOP

HIKES: D, O, W, L.
TOTAL DISTANCE, W: 18 Miles.
DIFFICULTY: Level II.
SEASON: July 4 — October 1.
USGS MAP: Snowyside.
USFS MAP: Sawtooth Wilderness Area (Sawtooth N.R.A.).
MILEAGE: 205 (2 Dirt).

INTRODUCTION: This is one of the most popular hikes in the Sawtooths, and justly so. The hike to Twin Lakes takes you to a mountain fairyland surrounded by rugged 10,000-foot peaks named McDonald, El Capitan, and Snowyside. And the trail to Twin Lakes is *the* perfect trail, a masterpiece of the art. Completing a loop route past Toxaway Lake takes you through some not-quite-so-extraordinary scenery, down a far-from-perfect trail. While the trail to Twin Lakes is well maintained, its five creek crossings make it Level II (or worse at high water levels). Likewise, the pass to Toxaway Lake and the loop return require Level II skills. This loop can be hiked clockwise or counterclockwise. If you get an early evening start, take the Toxaway Trail and camp in the Yellow Belly drainage just over the moraine. Otherwise, climb on the best trail to Twin Lakes.

THE TRAIL: Your goal is either Alice (5½ miles), Twin (6½ miles), or Toxaway Lake (9 miles). The hike to Twin is fairly level to the end of Pettit Lake, where there is some camping. Some gradual climbing and two crossings bring you to a steep stretch below a fabulous bench that lies below Parks Peak. This is a good goal for day-hikers. Continue climbing and crossing until you pass from the noise of the creek to the quiet of the lakes.

The lakes area is short on campsites. There are some by the lower ponds, a few at the far end of Alice, and many along the east side of Twin Lakes. The present trail from Alice to Twin differs from the one on the USGS map, climbing to a rise above the lakes rather than along the outlet stream. Good water can be found in the southwest corner of the Twin Lakes — a level area not recommended for camping because of its fragile vegetation.

The trail from Twin to Toxaway has also, mercifully, been rebuilt. It now climbs north from the trail divide above Twin Lakes and then cuts west to reach a notch in the ridge. This divide may hold snow into August. The trail descends to the right of a creek, crossing at last below a falls close to the level of Toxaway Lake. There are campsites from this to the next stream crossing. The Toxaway campground is just below the Edna Creek Trail junction.

The trail from Toxaway to the Yellow Belly flats is a poor relation to the Pettit Creek Trail. While it would be an excellent trail in the White Clouds, it is below average for the Sawtooths. It has many boggy stretches and a nasty habit of climbing when it should be dropping. There are only a few campsites on the descent to the flats, all on the margins of the lakes along the trail. Once in the lodgepole flats, there is abundant camping.

The trail over the moraine from there to Pettit Lake features climbing stretches with steep, washed-out pitches that will test your end-of-loop legs. The descent to Pettit Lake is on better trail.

EXTENSIONS: You can easily take a third day to do this loop, camping at both Twin and Toxaway Lakes. You can also use the two trails going north from Toxaway to reach other lakes.

ACCESS: Drive to Ketchum via I-84, US-20, and ID-75. Continue north, and 13½ miles past Galena Summit turn left on the Pettit Lake Road. Bear right after you cross Alturas Lake Creek, and turn right on the road to Tin Cup Transfer Camp. There are campsites at the trailhead, one mile in at the end of Pettit Lake, or 2 miles in at the Yellow Belly flats.

Alice-Twin-Toxaway loop, Pettit Lake Creek

ALPINE CREEK

HIKES: D, O, W.
TOTAL DISTANCE, W: 10 Miles.
DIFFICULTY: Levels I, III.
SEASON: June 15 — October 1.
USGS MAP: Snowyside.
USFS MAP: Sawtooth Wilderness Area
  (Sawtooth N.R.A.).
MILEAGE: 207 (1½ Dirt).

INTRODUCTION: The Alpine Creek Trail ends a mere 2½ miles up the valley, and from there the Level III hiker has his choice of three routes, each leading up a fork of the creek to a high lakes basin.

THE TRAIL: Day-hikers can hike the Level I maintained trail to the big meadow, while overnighters can stop at one of the many campsites that start just past the meadow. Weekenders have their choice of three basins, the preferred one being the north fork of the creek.

After you find the trail in the lodgepoles, go left. Two steep pulls bring you to a world of meadows where you can see several avalanche scars. Campsites begin in a wood past the big meadow where the trail passes next to the creek. Salmon spawn there, with trout swimming behind them to lap up stray eggs.

The trail becomes harder to follow in its last mile, bogging down from time to time. It passes several more campsites in the trees below the trail. The last meadow comes after a difficult boggy stretch. The maintained trail finally ends where it is pinched between the creek and the mountain.

The North Fork route follows a faint fisherman's trail to the lake at 8,522 feet, 5 miles from the trailhead. It goes right from the maintained trail's end, staying to the right of the creek as it climbs 1,000 feet to a high basin. The best campsites are by the 8,522-foot lake. From there you can hike to the upper lakes below Snowyside, which have no campsites.

The route to the center fork of Alpine Creek crosses the creek where the north fork route goes right. Stay to the left of this fork as you work your way to the big lake at 8,522. There are campsites at this lake and by the lakes above it.

The route up the southern fork of Alpine Creek is perhaps the most challenging of the three. Cross the main creek at the last meadow. Stay to the left of the south fork as you climb to a level area where a magnificent beaver dam has flooded an entire meadow. Stay left of the creek as it passes more meadow and climbs again. When the fork that drains the 8,700-foot lake takes off, switch to the right side of the creek and follow a poor trail to the lake at 8,251. You may camp by the pond that precedes the lake. The best route to the 8,700-foot lake leaves from here, passing good campsites at the two-pond divide. Turn left at the outlet creek and climb to the lake, where there are campsites.

ACCESS: Take I-84, US-20, and ID-75 from the Broadway overpass to Ketchum. Continue north 49½ miles to the Alturas Lake Road. Turn left and stay on the paved road, continuing straight on the road when it turns to dirt. The trailhead is on the right, just before a ford. You may camp in a Forest Service campground by the lake, or near the trailhead in the lodgepoles.

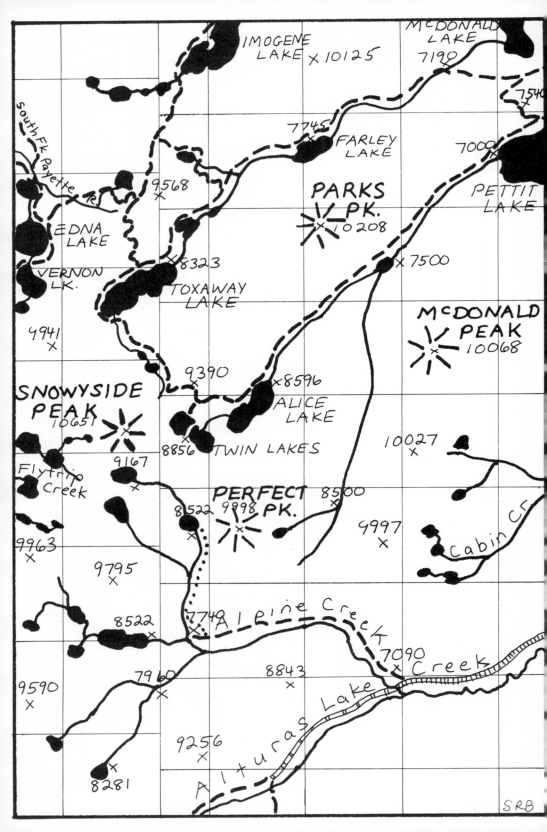

Alpine Creek Lakes — the hiker's reward

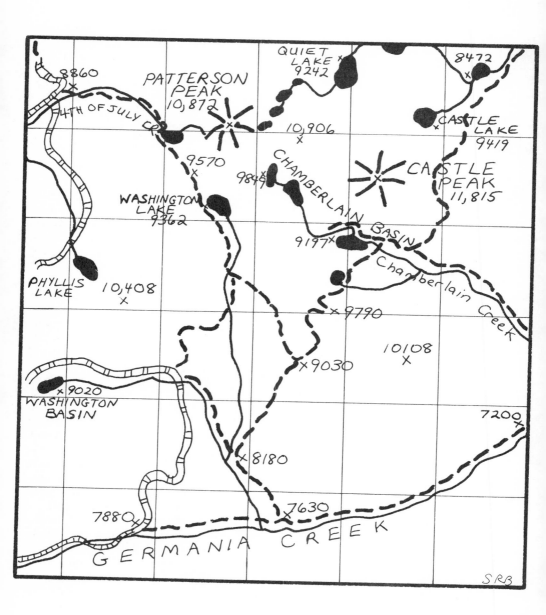

QUIET
LAKE ×
9242

8472
×

8860
×

PATTERSON
PEAK
10,872

CASTLE
LAKE
9419

F 4TH OF JULY CR.

10,906
×

9570

984 ×

CHAMBERLAIN

CASTLE
PEAK
11,815

WASHINGTON
LAKE
9362

9197 ×

CHAMBERLAIN BASIN

Chamberlain Creek

PHYLLIS
LAKE

10,408
×

× 9790

10108
×

× 9030

× 9020
WASHINGTON
BASIN

7200
×

× 8180

7880 ×

× 7630

GERMANIA CREEK

S.R.B

156

CHAMBERLAIN BASIN

HIKES: W, L.
TOTAL DISTANCE, W: 13 Miles.
DIFFICULTY: Level III.
SEASON: July 10 — October 1.
USGS MAPS: Boulder Chain Lakes, Galena Peak*, Horton Peak*.
USFS MAP: White Cloud-Boulder Mountains (Sawtooth N.R.A.).
MILEAGE: 208 (12 Dirt).

INTRODUCTION: Idaho has two Chamberlain Basins, the most famous of which is in the River of No Return Wilderness Area. This less-known area, in the White Clouds, lies a mere 2,700 feet below Castle Peak, the highest in the range. The trail to Chamberlain Basin is a typical White Clouds trail that proceeds directly to its destination without wasting time on such nonsense as switchbacks. Some sections of trail are so steep you could rappel down. Level III.

THE TRAIL: Day or overnight hikes are not recommended for this trail. The 6½ miles to the basin demand a full day each way, and there are no intermediate stopping points. You start by descending alongside Germania Creek. The trail goes up as well as down on its way to Washington Creek, passing a few campsites on both sides of the creek. You must ford Washington Creek, from which you should fill your canteen. A short distance beyond, your trail bears left and stays level, while the trail to the East Fork Salmon River descends to the right. After a steep initial climb, the trail levels off and passes some dry campsites. Like those along Germania Creek, these are susceptible to motorcycle noise and dust.

The trail to Chamberlain Basin is marked by welcome "No Motor Vehicles" signs. Parts of it may expand your consciousness of the word "steep." The trail meets the 4th of July trail and continues climbing, finally leveling off at the 9,400-foot level, where you may find close-to-water campsites with a view of Castle Peak. After you cross the summit you have a steep descent into Chamberlain Basin, which has many dispersed campsites. The trail passes to the right of the first lake, goes through a wood, and comes to the 9,197-foot lake. Go right and then left around the lake's north side. Climb along the right side of the inlet stream, and you will come to a large meadow just made for camping.

EXTENSIONS: The heart of the White Clouds lies north of Chamberlain Basin and can be reached via the pass just east of Castle Peak.

ACCESS: There are two dirt roads that leave Stanley Basin and head east into the White Clouds. The Pole Creek-Germania Creek Road is in better condition than the Fourth of July Creek Road, which is not saying much, but it should be passable by sedans. The Forest Service attempts to grade this road at least once a millenium. Drive to Ketchum via I-84, US-20, and ID-75. Drive north on ID-75 7 miles past Galena Summit, to the Pole Creek Road, immediately south of milepost 165, where you turn right. The Forest Service, using sophisticated natural resources management techniques, takes down this road sign just before busy weekends and replaces it afterwards. At the end of a long, level stretch, with campsites along Pole Creek, the road narrows and starts to climb with a vengeance. Four miles later you come to Pole Creek Summit. Current maps show the road after the summit to be worse than the road before, but it is probably better. Two fords, starting ¼ mile before the trailhead, will stop most passenger cars, but it is easy to hike on the north side of Germania Creek to the trailhead, where the road cuts left past a "Narrow, steep road" sign. There are campsites along the Germania Creek Road and Trail.

Chamberlain Basin — Castle Peak view

Area Six

SUN VALLEY AND EAST

Idaho's famous resort of Sun Valley and the adjacent town of Ketchum are surrounded by three of the state's highest mountain ranges. The Smoky Mountains, to the west, reach 10,000-foot elevations; the Boulder Mountains, to the north, reach 11,000 feet; and the Pioneers, to the east, reach 12,000 feet. Much of this country is roadless, and parts of all three ranges are being considered for wilderness designation.

These mountains are fairly well trailed. Most of the trails are steep, as they must reach 9,000-to-10,000-foot passes from 6,000-to-7,000-foot valleys. Altitude becomes a factor here, and the thin air takes a toll on flatlanders. Most of the trails are rugged, as the shaley rock of these mountains makes trail maintenance difficult. Switchbacks are at a premium, even on such 3,000-foot climbs as the one to West Pass. Many trails end rather than attempt to climb steep stretches, and few actually cross passes in the high Boulders and Pioneers. Some trails do offer easy hiking in the lower valleys.

Whether you stay in the sheltered valleys or venture into the remote high country, you will find rewarding hiking in the unique environment of these rugged mountains.

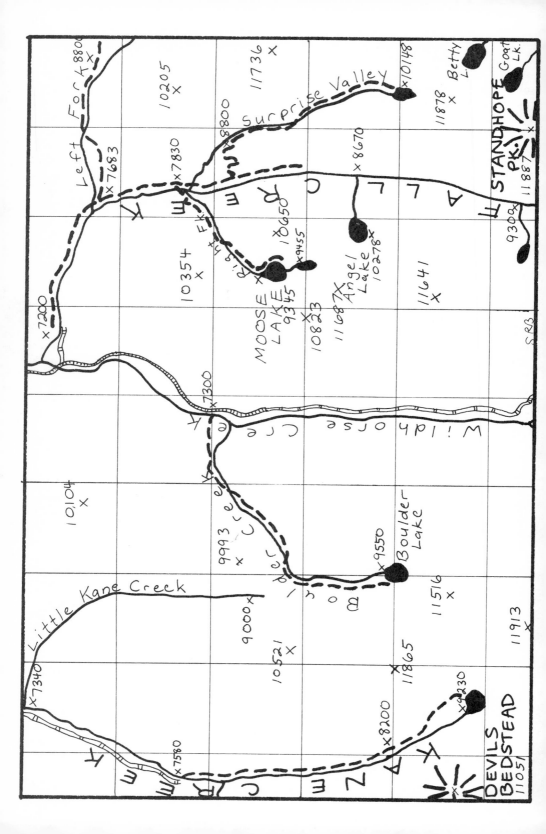

FALL CREEK

HIKES: D, O, W, L.
DIFFICULTY: Level I, II, III.
TOTAL DISTANCE, W: 12 Miles.
SEASON: June 20 — October 1.
USGS MAP: Standhope Peak.
USFS MAP: East Half Challis N.F.
MILEAGE: 179 (18 Dirt).

INTRODUCTION: Fall Creek occupies a fabulous valley flanked by 11,000-foot peaks of the Pioneer Mountains. The drainage, which offers superb hiking, is closed to motor vehicles. Level I hikers can stay in the lower valley, Level II hikers can climb to Moose Lake, and more advanced hikers can camp at Surprise Valley or upper Fall Creek.

THE TRAIL: Overnighters and day-hikers may hike to lower Fall Creek valley, 2½ miles in. Weekenders may opt for popular Moose Lake, 6 miles in, or the more secluded areas of upper Fall Creek or Surprise Valley. The trail's first stretch is an easy one on an old road. The only catch is that you must ford Fall Creek to reach the road. And the old creek can run mighty cold! After crossing, turn right on the road and follow it for 2 miles. The falls are off the road just south of the 7,666-foot mark on the USGS map. The descent from the hill brings you to the lower valley, where wooded areas offer excellent camping.

The old road ends and the trail begins at the Left Fork crossing. The Left Fork Trail, which looks rough, offers the only route out of the Fall Creek drainage and heads east toward the West Fork Big Lost River. The main trail heads south from the crossing. When it comes to Fall Creek it seems to cross but bears left instead. There is camping near here.

The Moose Lake Trail divide comes a mile past the Left Fork crossing. Bear right and look for a log upstream from the ford. The trail is well designed, with switchbacks of just the right gradient for climbing. When it finally starts to level off in a forest, it becomes a bit hard to follow. It stays to the right of the creek and appears again when it enters open country.

When it crosses the creek the trail leaves the shale behind and enters a zone of steep granite cliffs. After you have snaked through the granite the trail becomes more level, and you pass lush meadows on the right and possible campsites on the left. Moose Lake is surrounded by campsites and boasts outhouses and garbage cans.

Surprise Valley and upper Fall Creek offer more secluded camping than Moose Lake. The trails to these areas are well marked but poorly maintained.

ACCESS: Drive from Broadway Avenue on I-84 to Exit 95, US-20, and turn left. Drive to ID-75 and turn left again. Turn right at the stoplight in Ketchum (Trail Creek Road) and drive 21½ miles to the Copper Basin Road, where you turn right. Another 2 miles bring you to the Wildhorse Canyon Road, where you again turn right. The Fall Creek Road comes after 3½ miles. Turn left on it, and after ½ mile you will see the ford and the road-closure signposts across the creek. Park here and camp if you wish. Wildhorse Campground is just up the Wildhorse Canyon Road.

Fall Creek — Pioneers at dawn (Wildhorse Canyon)

162

NORTH FORK BIG WOOD RIVER

HIKES: D, O, W.
TOTAL DISTANCE, O: 6 Miles.
DIFFICULTY: Levels II, III.
SEASON: June 15 — October 1.
USGS MAPS: Amber Lakes, Ryan Peak.
USFS MAP: Ketchum Ranger District (Sawtooth N.F.).
MILEAGE: 163½ (5 Dirt).

INTRODUCTION: The North Fork of the Big Wood River is born in numerous creeks that drain the Boulder Mountains. These creeks descend by the waterfall route to strongly glaciated valleys. Elevations in the area reach 11,714 feet at Ryan Peak. There are hiking trails in many of the North Fork's tributaries, most of which vanish when they reach the valleys' ends and confront steep talus slides. Along the way they pass through rocky sagebrush slopes punctuated by intense level stands of forest that offer interesting camping. The rocky valley trails are Level II, while the approaches to the passes are Level III.

THE TRAIL: The North Fork can best be enjoyed by setting up a base camp near the West Pass Trail divide, 2½ miles in. From there you can day-hike the moderate Level II trail up the North Fork or the steep Level III trail to West Pass. Start by taking the trail to the right of the register box. Climb to reach a cool passageway overarched by trees and then descend to the second crossing. There is a nice crossing log upstream. A second crossing, which may have to be forded, follows a short rocky stretch on the stream's west side.

A level, mostly forested, area is not far from the second crossing. Here the North Fork meets its last major tributary, an unnamed creek that leads toward Ryan and Kent peaks. Since the North Fork already has an East Fork and a West Fork, perhaps this stream should be called the Last Fork. The woods by the Last Fork offer good base camp sites.

The West Pass Trail, which ascends the Last Fork drainage, is unsigned and hard to find. It starts beyond the Last Fork crossing, leaving the northeast end of a horseshoe meadow that is directly across the North Fork from a distinctive open drainage. The switchback stretch at the start of the trail is deceiving, for there are mighty few switchbacks to follow! As you climb you will see many waterfalls. The last 800 feet to West Pass (10,030 feet) is pure macho on poor trail. A well-anchored winter camping tent would let you spend a night here in the shadow of Ryan Peak.

The main North Fork Trail climbs at a much mellower rate, passing from densely wooded patches to open sagebrush slopes and back to trees again. This trail, too, has its share of waterfall vistas. The author was turned back near the third crossing by a stampeding (well, advancing . . .) herd of sheep. Older Forest Service maps show a switchback trail over the divide to Ibex Creek — you might try to locate it.

EXTENSIONS: The West Pass Trail will quickly drop you down to the East Fork Salmon River. If you have more time you might hike a different branch of the North Fork. The West Fork boasts Amber and Window lakes, while the East Fork Trail leads to the head of Trail Creek.

ACCESS: Drive to Ketchum via I-84, US-20, and ID-75. Drive 8¼ miles north on ID-75 to the Sawtooth National Recreation Area headquarters and turn right. Drive 3½ miles on the North Fork Road until you come to Camp Manupu. Turn left and scout out the stream crossing. It can be worse than it looks and may stop passenger cars. There is a foot crossing upstream, and it's only 1½ miles to the trailhead, so you can walk from here. There are campgrounds all along the North Fork Road, with some nice ones past the Manupu ford.

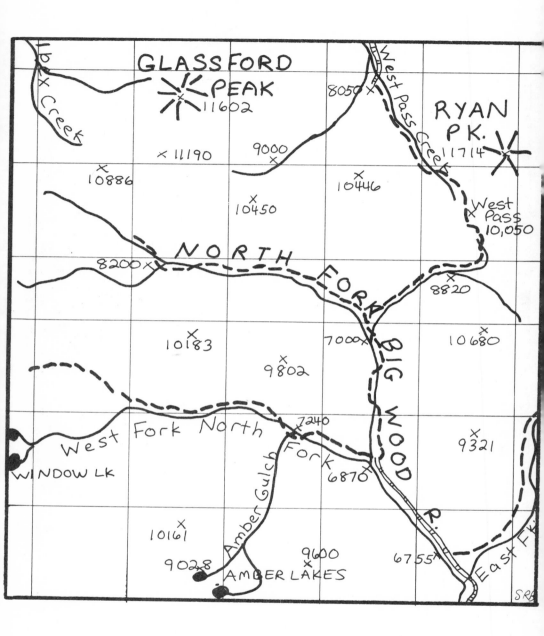

GLASSFORD PEAK
11602

Ibex Creek

× 11190

× 9000

8050 ×

West Pass Creek

RYAN PK.
11714

× 10886

× 10450

× 10446

West Pass
10,050

NORTH FORK

8200 ×

× 8820

× 10183

× 9802

7000 ×

BIG WOOD

× 10680

West Fork North Fork

7240

× 9321

WINDOW LK

Amber Gulch

6870

R.

× 10161

9028

9600

6755

East Fk.

AMBER LAKES

S.R.B.

164

North Fork of Big Wood River — water and rock

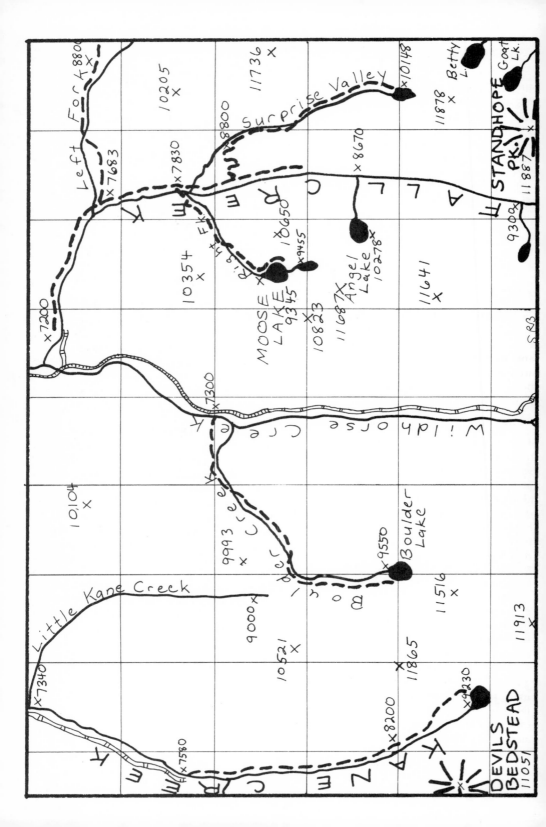

KANE LAKE

HIKES: D, O, W.
TOTAL DISTANCE, O: 9 Miles.
DIFFICULTY: Level III.
SEASON: July 10 — October 1.
USGS MAP: Phi Kappa Mountain.
USFS MAP: Ketchum Ranger District (Sawtooth N.F.), or East Half Challis N.F.
MILEAGE: 178 (15 Dirt).

INTRODUCTION: Kane Lake sits in a magnificent cirque basin. Peaks of the Pioneer Range tower 2,700 feet above it, and two waterfalls feed it. This popular area is not for everyone, though, because both the access road and the trail are very rough. This is Level III hiking.

THE TRAIL: Your goal is Kane Lake, 4½ miles in. The route begins with a ford of Kane Creek that can be tough in early season. Once across the creek you follow a jeep road for ½ miles. There are campsites along this stretch. At one point a trail sign directs you to the right, while the road bears left. Follow the road here, for the trail just bogs down in a meadow. The correct Kane Lake Trail bears right off the road a little later, when the road switches back to the left.

The trail is maintained for the next 2 miles and is fairly easy to follow. It meets the creek in a few places but never crosses it. At one of these meetings, next to a crystal clear pool, you come face-to-face with the Devils Bedstead. This would be a good day-hiker's destination (though many hardy souls make the round trip to the lake in a day). Past here the trail steeply climbs a hunk of rock only to descend again. The descent marks the end of the maintained trail.

For the next mile the route stays be-tween the streamside trees and the mountainside rocks. The departure from this fairly level stretch is abrupt. The trail makes a sharp left turn, climbing on a faint route that still keeps you between the trees and the rockslide. After climbing a while you get a good view of the falls just below Kane Lake. Here the trail disappears into a boulder field. Contour across it, and you will see the trail emerge and climb again.

You have a choice of routes here. You can pick your own trail through the slabby, semicliff-forming rocks and come out close to the lake and at its level. Or you can continue to climb to the left and come out above the lake level by some secluded campsites.

Kane Lake has many campsites — some in the lumpy meadows, some in the gnarled trees. It also has many fire rings, and there is no reason for making more. The steep terrain around the lake discourages travel except to the east. Climbing skills are essential in leaving the Kane Creek drainage.

ACCESS: Drive to Ketchum via I-84 from Broadway, US-20 from Exit 95, and ID-75 from its junction with US-20. Turn right at the stoplight in Ketchum and go past Sun Valley to Trail Creek Summit. Go 7 miles more and turn right on the Kane Creek Road. This tough, 5-mile road is not suitable for passenger cars. The National Park Service, in its report on a possible Sawtooths National Park, recommended closing the road to provide a buffer for Kane Lake (and probably to avoid maintaining it). You can camp at Forest Service campgrounds just over Trail Creek Summit or just across Kane Creek along the trail.

Niche at Kane Lake

PRAIRIE, MINER, AND NORTON LAKES

HIKES: D, O, W, L.
TOTAL DISTANCE, W: 13 Miles.
DIFFICULTY: Levels I, II, III.
SEASON: July 15 — October 1.
USGS MAPS: Baker Peak, Galena.
USFS MAPS: Ketchum or Fairfield Ranger
   Districts (Sawtooth N.F.).
MILEAGE: 176 (8 Dirt).

INTRODUCTION: The crest of the Smoky Mountains runs south from Galena Summit between Big Smoky Creek and the Big Wood River. Many of the peaks in the Smokies are over 10,000 feet high, and below their summits lie scenic lakes and incredible valleys. The trails in this area vary in quality. There are the well-maintained, popular Level I route to Norton Lakes; the steep Level II routes to Prairie Lake and from Miner to Norton; and the abandoned, Level III+ trail from Prairie to Miner.

THE TRAIL: The loop hike falls into three segments; from the trailhead to Prairie Lake, an easy weekend or hard overnight trip for Level II hikers (6 miles); from Prairie to Norton Lake, a very difficult Level III stretch (4 miles); and from Norton Lake to the trailhead, an easy day or overnight hike at Level I (3 miles).

From the trailhead register take the Bluff Creek Trail (a road for its first ½ mile) up the South Fork Norton Creek. There are possible campsites just before and after the first of the four creek crossings. The trail then crosses some tributary creeks, from which you should fill your canteens for the dry hike to Prairie Lake. Beyond the creeks the trail climbs at a steady, moderate rate through mixed meadows and forests. The 8,943-foot dome on your USGS map is readily visible, and there are dry campsites beyond it.

Take a right at the Prairie Lake Trail divide. The trail stays level for a while, passing more dry camps, and then climbs sharply. The steep slope and the high altitude make this a rugged climb, but there are sufficient rewards for reaching the ridgeline, a good day-hiker's goal. Below you lies Royal Gorge, before you the many peaks of the Fairfield Ranger District. Time passed here on map-and-compass work is well spent.

The trail to Prairie Lake remains highly scenic. It follows the left side of the ridge, then the right, and descends to the left. This is a hazardous stretch of trail hacked out of the side of a steep mountain and maintained infrequently. When you reach the level area at the head of Royal Gorge the trail disappears. Watch for an almond-shaped blaze. The climb to the divide is short and sassy, the descent off it the same. When you first see Prairie Lake, note the large meadow above and to the left of it. You may wish to camp here, or near Prairie Lake, or near the other lake at 8,701 feet. The Forest Service urges that you camp at least 100 feet from the lake.

The "trail" from Prairie Lake to Miner Lake is really a route, still reasonably well blazed but clearly not maintained in many years. It does an obvious thing — roughly contouring from Prairie (8,701 feet) to Miner (8,770 feet) — instead of descending 1,000 feet and then climbing. Since the terrain is not too difficult and there are many good game trails, you shouldn't worry if you find yourself off the blazed route. Just don't lose altitude unnecessarily! This Prairie-Miner Trail leaves the north end of Prairie Lake, where there are signs restricting motorized travel and lakeside camping. It passes a rock pile and a faint blaze and then goes along the north edge of a meadow next to the other 8,701-foot lake.

From here on you will encounter stretches with no blazes, with frequent blazes, and with multiple routes. Just resist the temptation to go down meadows and instead steadfastly contour, climbing whenever you must make a choice between up and down. There is one distinct drainage, which you should cross fairly high up. At last the trail turns the corner into the Miner Lake drainage and starts to climb at an alarming rate. After all, this trail is supposed to contour, right?

Just when you get disgusted with all the climbing, just after the trail climbs on a gravel wash for a while, and just when you get a good view of Norton Peak, watch for a puny blaze on a puny tree that shows the trail bears left. It climbs little from here on, and when you have a good view of the Miner drainage from the open area you can choose between continuing to contour, as some blazes indicate, or descending to cross a wet meadow and the creek to reach the Miner Lake Trail. There are few campsites around Miner, some on the

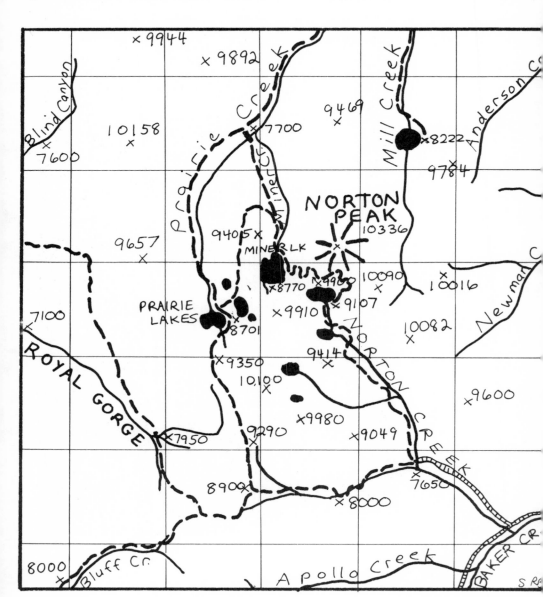

170

Lunch at Royal Gorge, Prairie-Miner-Norton loop

north and northwest end, a few possible ones to the south.

The trail from Miner to Norton climbs 1,100 feet to a 9,900-foot pass — the highest spot in this book. The trail is in very poor condition, and you must stay alert to follow it. It skirts the north end of the lake and then cuts right and climbs. Finding the first switchback is difficult but crucial. When the trail becomes hard to follow, look up and to your left, and you should see a blaze. From here the climb is steep and nasty, a good place to take it easy. The top is great for compass and camera work and for making snow cones. Norton Peak (10,336 feet) is just a hop, skip, and jump to the left. Start your descent to upper Norton Lake to the right and then switch back to the left to reach the area of the trees.

The descent from Norton Lakes to the trailhead follows a well-maintained, easy trail which has a 1,400-foot altitude gain. The rock formations in the valley are reminiscent of Utah or Colorado badlands. Try to avoid stepping on the toes of the many people who day-hike this trail and to avoid looking too smug (or exhausted) after successfully completing the scenic and challenging loop hike.

EXTENSIONS: A good loop goes left at the Prairie Lake-Bluff Creek Trail divide, descends Bluff Creek to Big Smoky Creek, ascends Big Smoky to Royal Gorge, and climbs back to the divide (a 2,200-foot climb).

ACCESS: Take I-84 from Broadway Avenue to Exit 95, US-20. Turn left and follow US-20 to ID-75. Turn left again on ID-75 and go 15 miles north of Ketchum to the Baker Creek Road. Go left and follow the road 6 miles to the Norton Creek Road. Turn right. The trailhead is 1½ miles in. There are many campsites along Baker Creek Road but none at the trailhead.

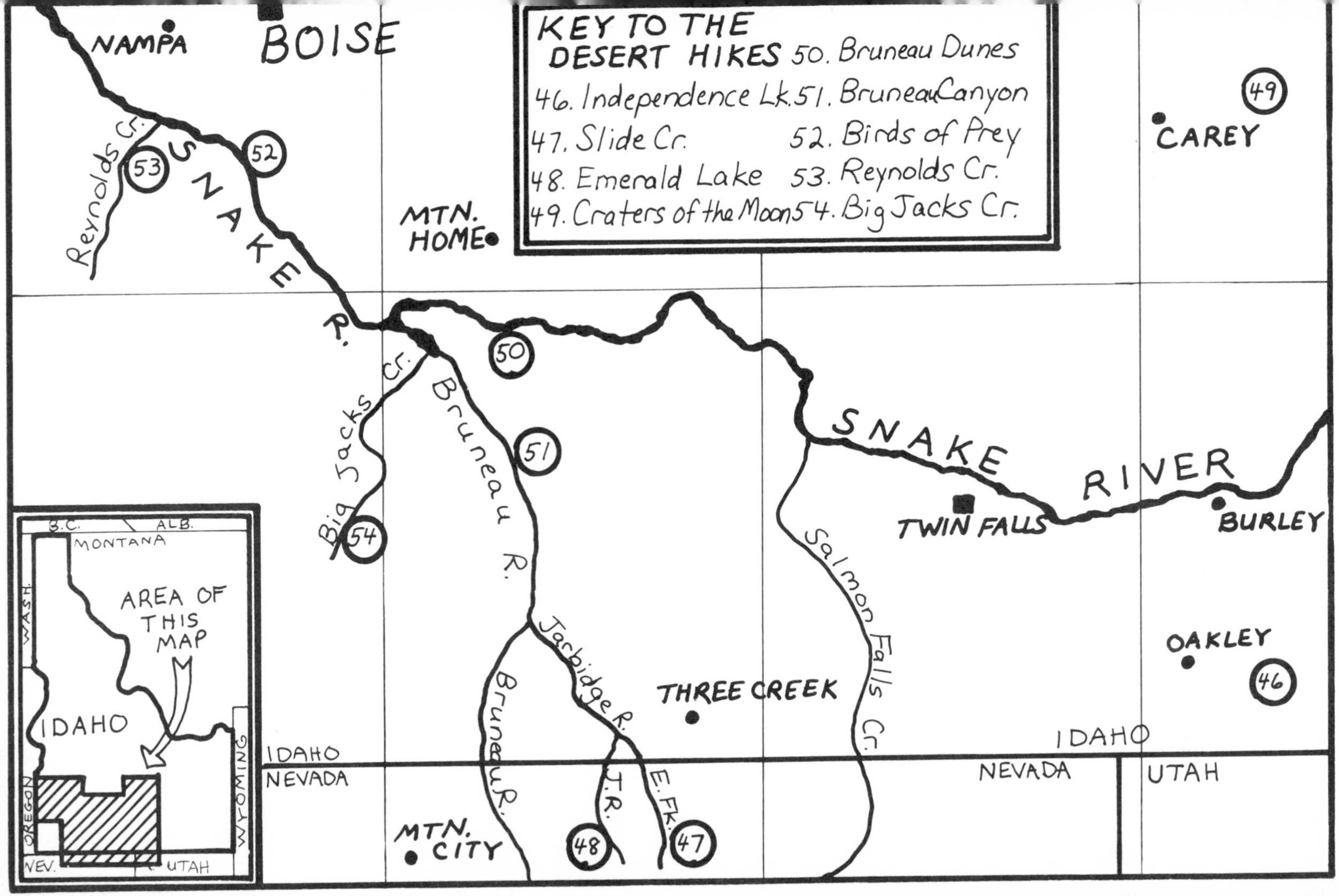
KEY TO THE DESERT HIKES
46. Independence Lk.
47. Slide Cr.
48. Emerald Lake
49. Craters of the Moon
50. Bruneau Dunes
51. Bruneau Canyon
52. Birds of Prey
53. Reynolds Cr.
54. Big Jacks Cr.
NAMPA
BOISE
MTN. HOME
CAREY
SNAKE R.
Reynolds Cr.
Big Jacks Cr.
Bruneau R.
SNAKE RIVER
TWIN FALLS
BURLEY
Salmon Falls Cr.
OAKLEY
THREE CREEK
Jarbidge R.
Bruneau R.
J.R.
E. FK.
MTN. CITY
IDAHO
NEVADA
UTAH
B.C.
ALB.
MONTANA
WASH.
OREGON
NEV.
WYOMING
AREA OF THIS MAP

Area Seven
THE DESERT GROUP

This group includes nine hikes — six in the desert and three in mountains that rise above it. The good guys in this section are the Forest Service, National Park Service, and Idaho State Department of Parks and Recreation. These agencies have marked and maintained desert hiking trails. The bad guys are the Bureau of Land Management.

The BLM administers most of Idaho's desert lands, as well as the Owyhee Mountains, but it has done little to encourage nonmotorized recreation. At present there is one mile of trail for every 59,378 acres of BLM land in Idaho. The BLM's wilderness study program will not be completed until 1991, though a few areas are receiving accelerated consideration. Hopefully, this new emphasis on wilderness will help the hiker. Now, however, almost every desert hike on BLM land involves several obstacles, including route selection and finding, water carrying, road access, and cattle and rattlesnake avoidance.

Some guidelines for carefree desert hiking are: Carry lots of water and *drink* it before you collapse; replace the salts you lose by perspiration; avoid hiking in the noontime heat; cover all skin with loose, lightweight cotton clothing; wear a hat that covers the back of the neck; carry sunglasses for conditions of extreme glare which can cause sunblindness; be aware of the flash-flood hazard; and carry a bandana for protection from possible dust storms.

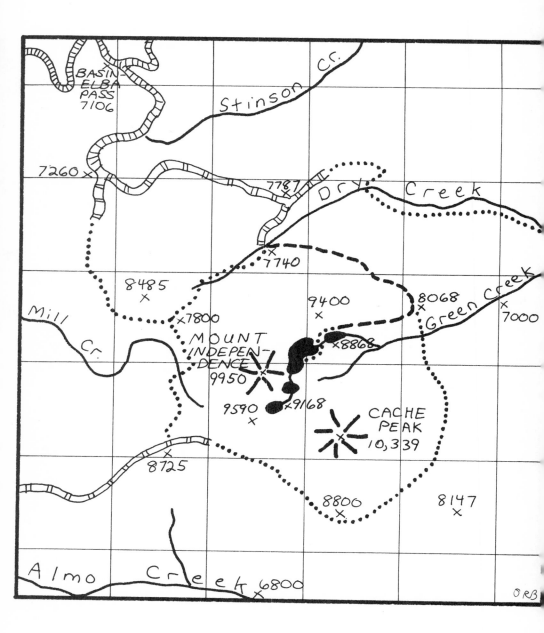

BASIN-
ELBA
PASS
7106

Stinson Cr.

7260 ×

7787 ×

Dry Creek

× 7740

8485
×

9400
×

8068
×

Green Creek

7000
×

Mill

Cr.

× 7800

MOUNT
INDEPEN-
DENCE

× 8868

9950
×

9590
×

× 9168

CACHE
PEAK
10,339
×

8725
×

8800
×

8147
×

Almo Creek 6800
×

O.R.B.

INDEPENDENCE LAKES

HIKES: D, O, W.
TOTAL DISTANCE, O: 7 Miles.
DIFFICULTY: Level I.
SEASON: July 15 — October 1.
USGS MAP: Cache Peak.
USFS MAP: Burley Ranger District (Sawtooth N.F.).
MILEAGE: 196 (10 Dirt).

INTRODUCTION: There are several good trails in the Minidoka Division of the Sawtooth National Forest. The best one leads to a high cirque basin under 10,339-foot Cache Peak, where Precambrian schists, quartzites, and marbles are exposed. The area, a true "island of green" in a sea of desert, was recommended for wilderness classification by RARE II. The trail to the first lake is really an old road and, despite a steep stretch, is Level I.

THE TRAIL: The overnighter's goal is the second of the four Independence Lakes, 3½ miles in. Day-hikers can stop ½ mile sooner at the first lake. Start this hike with a home-filled canteen. The trail is clearly marked and for the first 3 miles follows an old road. As it contours around the east side of the mountain it offers an outstanding view of Elba Basin and the Raft River Valley. There are a few campsites where the trail crosses a fork of Dry Creek just before it starts to climb. And climb it does — 800 feet in one mile. The Forest Service should replace this stretch of road with a nice switchback trail.

The cirque basin is a unique scenic area whose beauty has been protected by USGS bans on trail-bike riding and cattle grazing. Good campsites are scarce, because most of the level ground is studded with boulders. The best sites are closer to the lakes than strict wilderness rules would allow, and a groundcloth might help keep your tent dry. The second lake has the most campsites.

To make this a weekend hike, try climbing one of the peaks. The best route to them seems to leave the northwest corner of the last lake, climbing just below and to the right of a red rock outcrop and then cutting back to the left to reach the saddle between the two peaks.

EXTENSIONS: The USFS map shows a possible loop route, the Rangers Trail. There are no signs for this trail where it should cross Green Creek and head south, and the stretch that heads up Dry Creek from the trailhead is heavily grazed. Hopefully, wilderness designation will prompt the Forest Service to upgrade the trails and downgrade the grazing in this area.

ACCESS: Drive to Burley Exit 208 on I-84 from the Broadway overpass. Turn south on ID-27 and follow it until it ends in the middle of Oakley. Turn left and travel straight on the paved road for 8½ miles until it bears right. Your route goes straight, towards Elba. After a steep climb you come to Basin-Elba Pass. From here to the trailhead, about 5 miles, the road is rough. The Forest Service recommends against passenger car use, though careful driving can get a car to the trailhead. The route is poorly signed but can easily be followed by referring to the USGS map, which shows the entire route from Basin-Elba Pass. Bear right at the Stinson Creek sign, bear left at the Pot Holes turnoff, and turn right to Dry Creek when you are 4 miles from the pass. There is lots of parking and some camping in the trailhead area. On the way out you might want to go east to Elba and then south to City of Rocks, returning through Oakley.

Cliffs of marble — Cache Mountain

SLIDE CREEK

HIKES: D, O, W, L.
TOTAL DISTANCE, W: 14 Miles.
DIFFICULTY: Level II.
SEASON: June 5 — September 20.
USGS MAP: Jarbidge (1:62,500).
USFS MAP: Santa Rosa and Humboldt Divisions (Humboldt N.F.).
MILEAGE: 149 (77 Dirt) or 202 (17 Dirt).

INTRODUCTION: If America has a "forgotten" wilderness area, it is the Jarbidge. This northern Nevada area is far from population centers and does not offer the "ideal" scenery of glacial carved, granitic mountains. Yet it is close to Idaho (the only year-around roads to the area pass through Idaho), and its high volcanic mountains and beautiful desert valleys provide excellent hiking. The Slide Creek Trail gives an introduction to the full range of Jarbidge ecosystems, from coniferous forests to desert streamside woodlands. It takes you to the heart of the Jarbidge Wilderness Area, the East Fork Jarbidge River, on a good Level II trail.

THE TRAIL: Your goal is the East Fork, 7 miles in. Day-hikers and overnighters can stop around the sixth crossing, about 3½ miles in. To start, ignore the "trail" signs and follow the old road down to the draw. The wilderness boundary marker and check-in box are your guideposts. Just past them comes the first crossing of Slide Creek. A second and third soon follow. As you come to the fourth crossing look to your right. A number of semilevel campsites surround a beautiful series of beaver ponds, built by a master engineer who should have helped on the Teton Dam.

More beaver ponds, but not many campsites, lie downstream. As you continue to descend, you pass cliffs of Jarbidge rhyolite. (Why doesn't Idaho have more areas like this?) The fifth crossing is facilitated by a log downstream, but the sixth and seventh (close together) must be forded. This would be a good goal for day-hikers and overnighters, as there are campsites by the crossings. The trail now drops sharply to God's Pocket Creek, where there is more camping. The East Fork Jarbidge River is not much farther and has a large camping area by a pretty trout stream.

EXTENSIONS: The Slide Creek Trail leads to several different hikes. One excellent loop hike would start at Hummingbird Springs. Take the Divide Trail to the head of the East Fork, descend it to Slide Creek, then climb to the Pole Creek Guard Station. You could also just descend the East Fork to Robinson Hole.

ACCESS: There are two good routes, a longer one by pavement and a shorter one by dirt. The paved route follows I-84 for 83 miles from Broadway Avenue to Bliss (Exit 137), where you turn right on US-30. Follow US-30 for 40 miles to the junction with US-93, where you turn right. Go south for 23½ miles to the first Rogerson exit and turn right again. After ¾ mile take a right on a paved road. The Pole Creek Guard Station Road, where you turn left, is 36½ miles west of here. After 15 miles on the dirt road you come to the guard station turnoff, where you bear left and continue another mile to the Jarbidge Wilderness Road. Turn right, and then right again at the UC Corral Road. Go through the fence, bear left, and you will soon be at the trail sign. This area is grazed and offers poor camping. The Hummingbird Springs Road may have more camping.

The dirt road route uses the Bruneau Desert Road. Follow directions for Bruneau Canyon (page 189) as far as the Overlook turnoff, where you should continue straight. Follow signs for Three Creek, Rogerson, and Murphy's Hot Springs. Turn left when you come to the paved road and right on the Pole Creek Road after 3½ more miles.

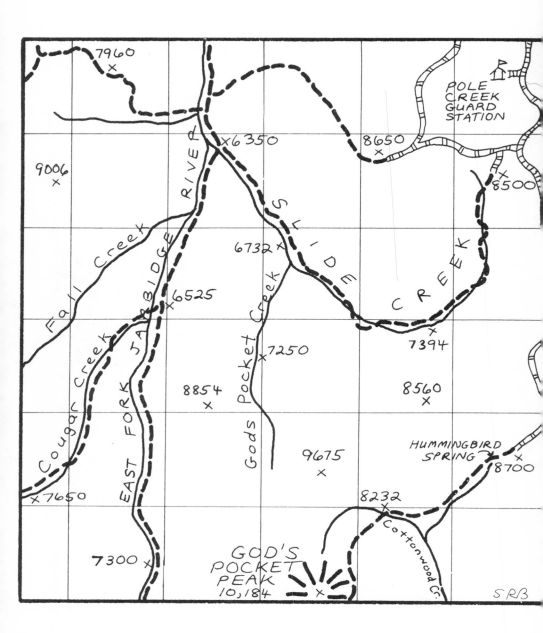

POLE
CREEK
GUARD
STATION

7960

×6350

8650

9006

8500

Fall Creek

JARBIDGE RIVER

SLIDE

CREEK

6732

6525

Gods Pocket Creek

7250

7394

Cougar Creek

8854

8560

EAST FORK

9675

HUMMINGBIRD
SPRING

8700

×7650

8232

Cottonwood Cr.

7300 ×

GOD'S
POCKET
PEAK
10,184

S·R·B

Slide Creek

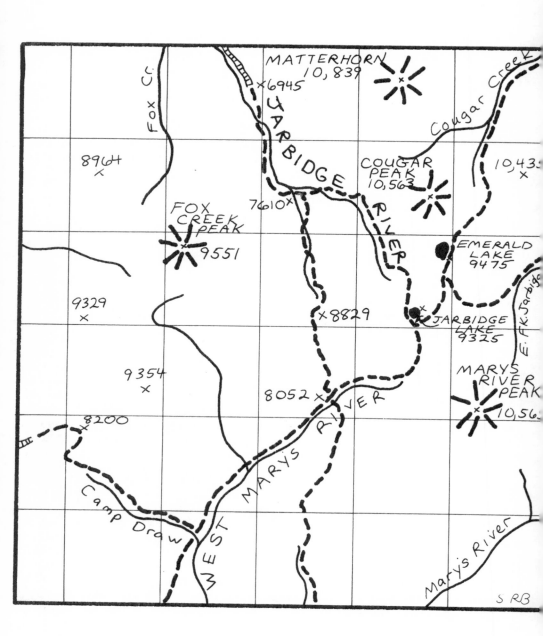

EMERALD LAKE

HIKES: D, O, W, L.
TOTAL DISTANCE, W: 16 Miles.
DIFFICULTY: Levels II, III.
SEASON: July 4 — September 20.
USGS MAP: Jarbidge (1:62,500).
USFS MAP: Santa Rosa and Humboldt Divisions (Humboldt N.F.).
MILEAGE: 216 (20 Dirt).

INTRODUCTION: This is the other major Jarbidge trailhead, and it offers excellent views of the major peaks and valleys. The first 6 miles are on trail that is being considered for addition to the Jarbidge Wilderness but is still open to trail-bike devastation. The trail is Level II as far as Jarbidge Lake and becomes Level III on the rocky route to Emerald Lake and on the loop route.

THE TRAIL: Your goal is Emerald Lake, a long 8 miles in. Day-hikers may stop near Perkins Cabin, 2½ miles in, and overnighters can find good campsites in the dry stream bed or at Jarbidge Lake, 5½ miles in. The trails are in good condition and are well signed — a good thing, since neither of your maps is very good! For the first 2½ miles you travel on an old mining road which only crosses the river once. There are few campsites on this stretch and few on the way to Jarbidge Lake. Where the road ends, the trail divides. To the right is the West Marys River Trail, which you may return on. To the left is the Jarbidge Lake Trail, which you want now. It quickly leaves the old road for a series of switchbacks. After a while you meet the road again, and here you must be alert because the trail goes left and crosses the river, leaving the road behind on the way to more switchbacks. At one point there

are meadows along the river course from which the river has vanished, only to reappear upstream. You may find a campsite here. When you next cross the stream you should fill your canteens, for the water in Jarbidge Lake probably isn't drinkable. There are many campsites around Jarbidge Lake, with sites in the trees preferred to sites in the meadow.

The division above Jarbidge Lake is a special one. It divides the Great Basin and the Columbia River drainage. The Marys River flows into the Humboldt, which never reaches an ocean. The Jarbidge's waters flow into the Bruneau, the Snake, and the Columbia on their way to the Pacific. At the divide turn left and climb on a rocky trail to the ridgeline. All those 10,000-foot peaks look tempting to the hiker who likes to "walk up" mountains. You could even follow the ridge until you are above Emerald Lake and then drop down. The trail is easier, though, descending in long lazy switchbacks and occasionally crossing an older, steeper trail going down to the same place. The trail to Emerald Lake is not the one shown on your 1943 topographic map but a new one blasted out of sheer rock that traverses the mountainside until it reaches Emerald Lake. As you near the lake you'll see an unsigned trail junction, with a trail heading downhill. This is the trail down the East Fork Jarbidge River, and it leads past the ledge with ponds that you see below, where there is camping. At Emerald Lake there are many tiny trout and few lakeside campsites. More room for camping can be found in the meadows above the lake.

You may take a different and tougher route out to make a loop. Go back to the Jarbidge-West Mary divide and instead of turing right to Jarbidge Lake, go left to West Marys River. At first the trail is in good condition, but after a while it becomes harder to follow. If you trust your instincts you'll probably do just fine. As there are fewer trees to blaze, rock cairns and upright posts mark the trail. A tricky point comes when you must pass just left of a distinctive stand of aspen.

A pair of posts signals your return trail,

Emerald Lake — Jarbidge Peaks, all in a row

which heads north to the pass at 8,829 feet. Go right and climb straight up the ridge until you see the trail leading off to your left. (The switchback shown on your USGS map has disappeared since 1943.) Despite being poorly maintained, the trail is not hard to follow because it climbs on dry open slopes and stays to the right of the drainage. When you see a nice green meadow go right, and you will soon be at the pass. Across the pass are the nicest campsites of the whole hike. Bear left at first and follow the trail, not the old road. The trail has switchbacks, the road doesn't.

EXTENSIONS: The West Marys Trail can take you to the least-visited part of the wilderness, the Lost Draw-Willow Creek area. It also connects with the Marys River.

ACCESS: All roads lead to Jarbidge, or so it seems. There are five different routes. Three are reached by ID-51 south of Mountain Home. They are the Grasmere-Rowland Road, the Charleston Road, and the Gold Creek Road. The Rowland Road leads from Grasmere to Rowland and up the hill to the Gold Creek Road and then on to Jarbidge. It is rough and recommended for pickups only. The Charleston Road is a highly scenic one that opens around the Fourth of July. It leaves Nevada-51 about 10 miles south of Wildhorse Reservoir and heads east to the headwaters of the Bruneau River, then turns north and climbs over two 8,400-foot summits that offer good views of the Jar-

bidge Range before descending to the Jarbidge River south of town. The Gold Fork Road is open early in April and throughout the spring offers beautiful views of snowy mountains and grassy meadows. Take Exit 90 off I-84, the first Mountain Home exit. Go through town, through the underpass, and right on ID-51 at the stoplight. After a long mile turn left on ID-51 and go south for 111 miles to the Gold Fork Road, which goes left off Nevada-51 after you come to Wildhorse Reservoir. (Five miles south of Mountain City you pass a USFS ranger station where you can get current information and maps.) Two miles past Big Bend Campground bear right and follow the narrow, winding Meadow Creek Road to the Bruneau River. After you climb above the Bruneau you come to Rowland junction. Bear right for the Jarbidge River, and when you get there turn right for Jarbridge town. Go straight through town, and just after you cross the third bridge bear left on the Pine Creek Campground Road. (The Charleston Road meets the river here.) The trailhead is about 2½ miles up the road and has ample parking but no camping.

The other routes to Jarbidge are much more pedestrian. They are basically those you followed to Slide Creek. Go to Rogerson, head west on the paved road, and continue on it after it becomes a dirt road. Go past Murphy's Hot Springs and down Jarbidge Canyon through town to the trailhead. Or you can take the Bruneau Desert Road to the Rogerson-Jarbidge Road, turn right, and head for Jarbidge.

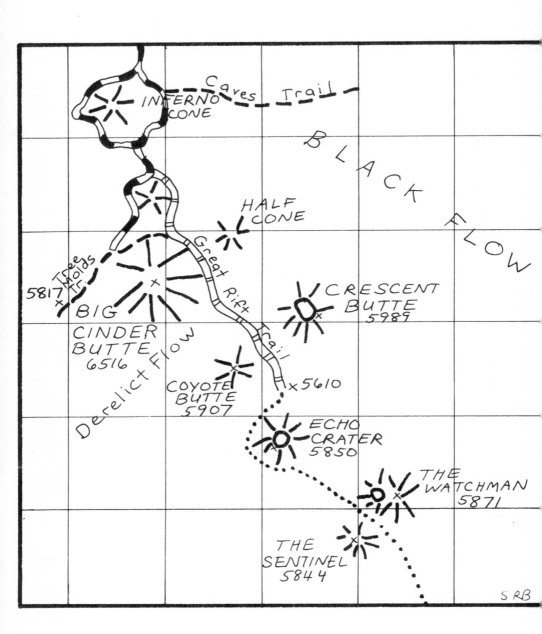

INFERNO CONE

Caves Trail

BLACK FLOW

HALF CONE

Tree Molds Tr.

5817
+ x

BIG CINDER BUTTE 6516

Great Rift Trail

CRESCENT BUTTE 5989

Derelict Flow

COYOTE BUTTE 5907

x 5610

ECHO CRATER 5850

THE WATCHMAN 5871

THE SENTINEL 5844

S RB

CRATERS OF THE MOON

HIKES: D, O, W.
TOTAL DISTANCE, O: 16 Miles.
DIFFICULTY: Levels I, III.
SEASON: April 20 — October 20.
USGS MAPS: Craters of the Moon National Monument (1:31,680), or Inferno Cone, The Watchman* (both 1:24,000).
NATIONAL PARK SERVICE MAP: See "Craters of the Moon" pamphlet.
MILEAGE: 151½ (No Dirt).

INTRODUCTION: The astronauts who trained at Craters of the Moon must have been dissatisfied when they landed on our planet's satellite. While Craters of the Moon is a warm, living, colorful area, the Moon is a cold, dead, gray place. It is necessary to get out in the backcountry of the monument at the right time to fully appreciate it. The car-bound tourists' trails don't put you in touch with the area's natural setting, and the midsummer heat can discourage even the roughest, toughest, most trail-hardened backpackers. It is best to explore the monument from early May to mid-June, the height of the flower season, or in September and October, when things have cooled off. As long as you stay on the trail you will enjoy fun, Level I hiking. Once off the trail everything is Level III.

Permits are required for travel in the 43,243-acre Craters of the Moon Wilderness Area. They can be obtained at the visitor center in person or by mail from the superintendent. There *are* waterholes as shown on the map, but these may take a long time to locate. The desert hiker's rule is one gallon of water per person per day, and you should not count on help from the waterholes in meeting this need. There are no rattlesnakes in the wilderness area because the lava is hard on their bellies and the temperature extremes are difficult to adjust to. You might wish to take an extra groundsheet for your tent, as the ground here is generally very rough. Several good natural history pamphlets are available for sale at the Monument headquarters.

THE TRAIL: The overnighter's goal is a camp near the Sentinel, 8 miles in. Echo Crater, 3½ miles in, makes a good day-hiker's or lazy overnighter's goal. Navigation in the backcountry is simple because Big Cinder Butte is an excellent landmark. To start, climb to a summit with a trail divide and go left on the Wilderness Trail. The next stretch, over a pahoehoe flow, is great fun. Well-spaced cairns lead all too soon to a cinder road which is your highway to the distant buttes. There are not as many good campsites along the road as you might think — it is hard to find the right combination of level ground and shelter from the sun and wind.

As the road passes to the west of Echo Crater it becomes fainter. However, it stays easy to follow, though exasperatingly curvy, all the way to the Sentinel. If you get restless on the way back, cut left off the road between Echo Crater and Coyote Butte. Head west-northwest across Derelict Flow to the Tree Molds Trail, which takes you back to your starting point. Deer trails and deer are everywhere along this route. The Derelict Flow is aa lava — nasty stuff that's hard on boots and ankles. It's too bad the deer can't be hired as guides for this stretch.

EXTENSIONS: Very few people reach the southeast corner of the wilderness area. Consult with the Park Service before you try it.

ACCESS: Take I-84 from the Broadway overpass to Exit 95, US-20. Turn left and follow US-20 all the way to Carey, 104 miles. Turn left at the junction with US-93 and US-26, and follow these roads 26 miles to the Craters of the Moon entrance. The visitor center, where you fill your canteen, is to the left. Take the Loop Drive from the center for 3½ miles, and turn right at the "Tree Molds-Wilderness Trails" sign. This road leads 1¼ miles to a large parking area. There is no camping here, and you must either use the campground near the visitor center or hike past the pahoehoe flow to the old road.

Sunset silhouette of Craters of the Moon

FIVE DESERT DAY HIKES

Sand Dunes Hiking Trail

TOTAL DISTANCE: 5 Miles.
DIFFICULTY: Level I.
SEASON: April 1 — October 30.
USGS MAP: Indian Cove* (1:62,500).
STATE PARK PAMPHLET: Sand Dunes
   Hiking Trail.
MILEAGE: 61 (No Dirt).

THE TRAIL: The trail, in Bruneau
Dunes State Park, is a route marked by
eight posts. The best time to hike it is
early in the morning, before the ever-
present winds obliterate the story etched
in sand of the previous night's activity.
Start at the visitor center, where you can
pick up a trail guide, and head south along
the fence line. Once past a large marshy
area, bear left and aim for the high point
on the sand dune. When you reach the
dune's base, turn left and walk along the
lakeshore. A bad stretch comes when you
must skirt a small bay of the lake on the
back side of the dune. Continue around
the lake past the picnic area and across the
road. The visitor center soon comes into
view.

ACCESS: Take I-84 from Broadway to
Exit 90, the first Mountain Home exit. Go
through town and turn right on ID-51 just
beyond the underpass. After 1¼ miles turn
left on ID-51 and go south on it for 14
miles, where you turn left on the road to
the park. The park entrance comes in a
few miles and is well marked. Overnight
camping in the park is restricted to the
campground.

Bruneau Canyon

TOTAL DISTANCE: 2 Miles.
DIFFICULTY: Level II.
SEASON: April 1 — October 30.
USGS MAP: Winter Camp (1:62,500).
MILEAGE: 84 (15½ Dirt.)

THE TRAIL: Bruneau Canyon may be
the most beautiful spot in Idaho's desert.
Access into the canyon is limited. A poor
trail, no longer maintained, switchbacks
down to an old gauging station on the
river. Once down in the canyon you have
shade or sun, sand or sagebrush, muddy or
clear water to amuse you. And rattlesnakes
— don't forget the rattlesnakes!

ACCESS: Drive east on I-84 from the
Broadway overpass to the first Mountain
Home exit. Drive 4½ miles through town
and turn right on ID-51 just beyond the
underpass. After a long mile turn left on
ID-51. Drive 24 miles south and turn left
on the Bruneau Canyon Road. After 7½
miles the pavement turns right, but you
want to go straight on the dirt road. After
another 5½ miles bear right on the road
for Murphy's Hot Springs. After 2½ more
miles turn right on the Overlook Road.
Your turnoff comes 2¼ miles later and
goes left for 2¾ miles to a poor road,
where you turn right. The rim is another
2¾ miles down this road.

Desert day hikes — Bruneau Canyon

Snake River Birds of Prey Natural Area

TOTAL DISTANCE: 4 Miles.
DIFFICULTY: Level II.
SEASON: May 15 — October 30.
USGS MAP: Oreana (1:62,500).
BLM PAMPHLET: Snake River Birds of Prey Natural Area.
MILEAGE: 31¼ (20½ Dirt).

INTRODUCTION: The Birds of Prey Natural Area is unique to North America and possibly to the world. Some 600 pairs of raptors nest here, including golden eagles; prairie falcons; red-tailed, ferruginous, marsh, and Swainson's hawks; American kestrels; turkey vultures; barn, great horned, short-eared, screech, burrowing, and long-eared owls; and ravens. Other visitors to the canyon include bald eagles, peregrine falcons, osprey, and more hawks. The outcome of a government plan to protect the food supply of these birds is embroiled in controversy at the present. Hikers in this area *must* respect the birds' need for privacy. Disturbed birds will abandon not only nests with eggs but also nests with young in them. You must avoid any area where your presence seems to make any bird uncomfortable. You must not linger along the canyon rim (nests are often just below it). Avoid the area's few trees, which are often used as nesting sites, and *stay out* of the area until at least May 15, when young birds are in less danger of being abandoned.

THE TRAIL: There are two good hiking areas on the north side of the Snake. One is the circular basin about 2½ miles south of Swan Falls Dam. The other is a fishhook-shaped drainage about 5 miles south-southeast of the dam. The Red Trails reach the circular basin's south side, and this approach is preferable to dropping over the east rim. Once in the basin you can find your own route down to the river.

An easy-to-follow old road leads from the head of the fishhook-shaped drainage down to the river. The trick is in getting to the head of the drainage. After the "Road Closed" sign, take a right at the road divide below the power lines. When this road descends to the right between two rock outcrops it comes to another junction, where you go straight. Walk on the right of a small drainage for a while and then take two lefts to the spot where the road enters the canyon, by some fence posts.

ACCESS: Start at the Meridian exit on I-84 — by taking the exit. Turn south on ID-69 and drive 7 miles to a sharp right in the road. Go right for 1 more mile to Kuna. Where the road bears right, you go straight and then take a left on Linder Road (Swan Falls Road). Follow this road 19 miles to a large transformer (being careful to make the sharp left turn that comes after 13 miles). Take the dirt road immediately to the left of the transformer. This is a horrible road, left that way to discourage use of the area. It should not be attempted when muddy or wet. The Red Trails hike starts when you cross a creek bed 2 miles in. Hike across the desert to the rock cairn on the canyon rim and follow the rim to the Red Trails. The other hike starts 1½ miles further down the road, where a road leading to the right has a "Road Closed" sign and where the powerlines on the left make a turn.

Reynolds Creek

TOTAL DISTANCE: 3 Miles.
DIFFICULTY: Level III.
SEASON: April 1 — October 15.
USGS MAP: Wilson Peak.
MILEAGE: 27½ (5 Dirt).

THE TRAIL: Reynolds Creek cuts a fine gorge through the northern Owyhee Mountains. For 8 miles of its path it is neither trailed nor roaded, and the BLM is studying it for wilderness designation. The first mile is the most spectacular, with rugged cliffs on either side of the creek. Beyond there the canyon widens a bit, and the cow pies become very thick. Start by descending into the bowl and then bear right for the creek. Cross it if you can, for the west side trail is better. If you can't cross due to high water, follow an irrigation ditch to its end and then climb the bank to an old road which makes for good hiking. When this road peters out you are on your own. There are short stretches of trail on the sagebrush flats but also many rough, rocky, trailless places. After you see a drainage enter from the west, the canyon widens. Unless you fancy evidence of bovine activity, this is the place to stop.

ACCESS: Drive to Exit 38 on I-84, 6 miles west of the Meridian interchange. Turn left and drive through Nampa, following signs for Murphy and getting on ID-45. Cross the Snake River at Walter's Ferry and go straight on a paved road when the highway bears left, 21½ miles from Exit 38. Turn right on ID-78 and go 2½ miles to milepost 17, where you turn left. Pass to the left of a cemetery and take the left forks that come 1 and 2½ miles from the highway. At last you see some old ruins (4 miles from the highway). Drive past them on the right and take a hard right turn. Go straight on this road to the trailhead, where you look down on a bowl to the left.

Big Jacks Creek

TOTAL DISTANCE: 5 Miles
DIFFICULTY: Level III.
SEASON: May 1 — October 15.
USGS MAP: Hill Pasture.
MILEAGE: 98½ (10½ Dirt).

THE TRAIL: In early spring you can view the scenic canyon of Big Jacks Creek by hiking down Duncan Creek. Later in the year, when its flow has lessened, you can hike along Big Jacks Creek as part of a loop route. To start the loop, cross Duncan Creek and climb up the ridge to a road divide. Bear right and descend to Jacks Creek near Holman Cabin. Once in the canyon, travel becomes difficult. Jacks Creek must be crossed at least eight times on your way down to Duncan Creek, and when you aren't crossing the creek you're threading your way along brushy cowpaths. Make sure you are on the south side of the creek when you arrive at the confluence of the two creeks. Duncan Creek has a more open canyon that is easier to travel, and, although you still face several stream crossings Duncan is a much smaller creek than Big Jacks and they are not so difficult. If you hike down Duncan Creek in the spring, go up Big Jacks Creek a short distance from the confluence to better view its canyon.

ACCESS: Drive 36 miles east on I-84 from Broadway Avenue to the first Mountain Home exit, where you turn right. Drive through town and turn right on ID-51 beyond the underpass. After a long mile turn on ID-51. Go south for 21¼ miles and bear left for Elko. After 24½ more miles a dirt road appears on the right. Take it and drive 7 miles, passing Wickahoney, until you see a poor road leading to the right. After 1¼ miles on this road it becomes too rough for passenger cars. The Buncel Place, the trailhead, is 2½ miles farther down the road, which should present no problem to pick-ups.

APPENDIX A

ADDRESSES

Forest Supervisor
Boise National Forest
1075 Park Blvd.
Boise, ID 83706

Forest Supervisor
Challis National Forest
Challis, ID 83226

Forest Supervisor
Payette National Forest
McCall, ID 83638

Forest Supervisor
Sawtooth National Forest
1525 Addison E.
Twin Falls, ID 83301

Sawtooth National Recreation Area
Ketchum, ID 83340

Forest Supervisor
Humboldt National Forest
976 Mountain City Highway
Elko, NV 89801

Superintendent
Craters of the Moon National Monument
Box 29
Arco, ID 83213

Bruneau Dunes State Park
Star Route, Box 41
Mountain Home, ID 83647

Bureau of Land Management
Boise District
230 Collins Rd.
Boise, ID 83702

Idaho Department of Fish and Game
600 South Walnut
P.O. Box 25
Boise, ID 83707

Idaho Division of Tourism and Industrial
    Development
Room 108, Capitol Building
Boise, ID 83720

U.S. Geological Survey
Branch of Distribution
Box 25286 Federal Center
Denver, CO 80225

Idaho Bureau of Mines and Geology
University of Idaho
Moscow, ID 83843

APPENDIX B

BIBLIOGRAPHY

Natural History

Alt and Hyndman. *Roadside Geology of the Northern Rockies.* Missoula, MT: Mountain Press, 1972.

Brown, Yocum, and Starbuck. *Wildlife of the Intermountain West.* Healdsburg, CA: Naturegraph Publishers, 1958.

Burleigh, Thomas D. *Birds of Idaho.* Caldwell, ID: Caxton Printers, 1971.

Davis, Ray J. *Flora of Idaho.* Dubuque, IA: Wm. C. Brown Co., 1952.

Larsen and Schmidt. *A Reconnaissance of the Idaho Batholith and Comparsion with the Southern California Batholith.* U.S. Geological Survey Bulletin 1070-A, 1958.

Linder and Fichter. *The Reptiles of Idaho.* Pocatello, ID: Idaho State University Press, 1970.

Parsons, Donna L. *Idaho: An Outdoor Classroom.* Nyssa, OR: Blue Star Publishing, 1968.

Ross, Clyde P. *Geology along U.S. Highway 93 in Idaho.* Moscow, ID: Idaho Bureau of Mines and Geology, 1963. (This book covers ID-75 through the Stanley Basin.)

Ross and Savage. *Idaho Earth Science.* Moscow, ID: Idaho Bureau of Mines and Geology, 1967

Recreation

Bureau of Land Management. *Idaho Recreation Guide.* Boise, ID: n.d.

Idaho Department of Parks and Recreation. *Idaho Outdoor Recreation Plan.* Boise, ID: 1978.

Backpacking

Fear, Eugene H., ed. *Outdoor Living.* Tacoma, WA: Tacoma Mountain Rescue, n.d.

Fletcher, Colin. *The Complete Walker.* New York: Alfred A. Knopf, 1968.

Hart, John. *Walking Softly in the Wilderness: The Sierra Club Guide to Backpacking.* San Francisco: Sierra Club Books, 1977.

Manning, Harvey. *Backpacking: One Step at a Time.* New York: Vintage, 1972.

McCarten, C. B., "Son of Iodine, Out of Halazone," *Wilderness Camping,* Volume 8 Number 4, December/January 1979, pp. 56-73. (Excellent article on water purification.)

Rethmel, R. C. *Backpacking.* Minneapolis, MN: Burgess Publishing Co., 1968.

APPENDIX C

EQUIPMENT CHECKLIST

The Ten Essentials
  Maps
  Compass
  Flashlight
  Extra Clothing
  Sunglasses
  Waterproofed Matches
  Fire Starter
  Extra Food
  Pocket Knife
  First Aid Kit

Basics
  Backpack
  Tent
  Sleeping Bag
  Foam Pad
  Rain Parka or Poncho
  Down or Dacron Parka
  Wool Shirt or Sweater
  Wool Hat
  Bandana
  Socks and Spare Socks
  Boots
  Long Pants
  Long-sleeved Shirt
  Stove (Filled)
  Cook Kit
  Ditty Bags for Food
  Canteen

Extras
  Day Pack
  Ground cloth
  Rain Pants
  Down or Dacron Vest
  Gloves or Mittens
  Sun Hat
  Towel
  Moccasins
  Shorts
  T-shirt
  Extra Fuel for Stove
  Grill for Fires
  50 Feet ⅛'' Nylon Cord
  Collapsible One-Gallon Jug

More Extras
  Garden Trowel
  Toilet Paper
  Ice Axe or Hiking Staff
  Insect Repellent
  Suntan Lotion
  Sewing Kit
  Thermometer
  Fishing Tackle
  Snakebite Kit
  Book
  Nature Guides
  Whistle
  Binocular/Monocular
  Camera/Extra Film